A
Layered
Life

Breaking Barriers *as a* Trailblazing
Black Woman *in* Corporate America

Gladys H. DeClouet

RIVER GROVE
BOOKS

This book is a memoir reflecting the author's present recollections of experiences over time. Its story and its words are the author's alone. Some details and characteristics may be changed, some events may be compressed, and some dialogue may be re-created. The names and identifying characteristics of some persons referenced in this book have been changed to protect their privacy.

Published by River Grove Books
Austin, TX
www.rivergrovebooks.com

Distributed by River Grove Books

Design and composition by Greenleaf Book Group and Jonathan Lewis
Cover design by Greenleaf Book Group and Jonathan Lewis
Cover image of *Black Enterprise* magazine on page 86: Copyright (c) 2009 by Earl G. Graves Publishing. Used with permission.
Photograph of the author and her granddaughters on page 87: Copyright (c) 2017 by photographer unknown.

Publisher's Cataloging-in-Publication data is available.

Print ISBN: 978-1-966629-45-0

eBook ISBN: 978-1-966629-60-3

First Edition

Contents

1

Pull the Thread

Ever pull on a small thread hanging from your sweater? What could go wrong? A quick tug and everything will look better—but the thread keeps unraveling. One thing leads to another, and, before you know it, you've nearly destroyed your entire garment, or as in my case, your entire life.

At some point, you cut the string before it gets any worse, but my sister and I weren't at that point yet, so we kept pulling, we kept talking. What she said to me and what I said to her would change us both forever. I had not answered her first question, so Dee repeated it.

"Did he ever, you know, go in your panties and penetrate you?"

"No," I said. "He never did. He was just always putting me up against the wall, and, and—rubbing, touching, and stuff like that." I could barely get the words out.

The silence was now on her end. "Hello?"

"I'm here," Dee responded.

It seems my answer was more than an answer. It opened the door to a much deeper, darker conversation, one neither of us was prepared to have. I had never told her my story because I thought it would hurt her. She had never told me hers because she figured it would hurt me. We were finally talking, and I found myself debating whether we both should have kept quiet.

It was hard to accept I was having this phone conversation now, in my sixties. This was supposed to be a simple call, no more, no less. I had a few questions about our childhood days growing up together in Jacksonville, Florida, but unanswered questions led to other unanswered questions.

My retirement has allowed more time for reflection. Retirement has me seeking for answers. Those days of endless corporate meetings and tight travel schedules are long gone. Things are quieter now.

This phone call was sobering because my secrets have been out of reach for decades. I placed them neatly in my mental hideaway. A place I call "the box." But time does weird things. Everything good and everything bad is leaking out now. I guess even secrets get tired of hiding.

The more Dee and I talked, the more I remembered. But still, I'm old-school. I believe there are certain things you just don't speak about, especially when they involve people you love. The circumstances surrounding my molestation was one of them. I put that to bed over fifty years ago, and, as far as I was concerned, it could stay there forever in silence.

But God had other plans—plans for me to come face-to-face with hurtful, damaging personal experiences so others can find the courage to do the same in their own lives. He has plans for me to share my personal and professional journey so young Black girls and women who dare to break new ground in their unique industries can know someone who walked the path before them. My journey is also a story of courage, leadership, and faith for anyone facing adversity or just the problems that life will inevitably present, regardless of one's gender, race, or religious background. Life comes in layers for everyone.

I have experienced unique blessings and opportunities. Mine is a story of optimism for anyone born into an environment where resources are few. People need to know that anything, and I do mean anything, is possible when you believe in yourself, secure your education, and never quit.

Young girls who come from where I come from have certain expectations placed on them. None of these expectations involve success in the ultraconservative good-old-boy network known as the oil industry, a very white, wealthy, and deeply protected business. Nor does it include success in the highest ranks of the restaurant industry. Now, add to that the fact that I did not have a pedigree, Ivy League background, or legacy relationships, and corporate success seemed to be a far-fetched dream. However, it is a dream I realized. Now, it's simply time to tell it all.

On September 28, 2021, my twenty-nine-year-old stepson died. This triggered me to stop procrastinating and write the book you are now reading, and to write it honestly without padding the sharp edges of my experiences. His death triggered me to slowly reach into "the box" and pull out parts of me that most of the people who know me have never seen.

My initial instinct was to play it safe with this book and protect the privacy of my personal life. I would rather discuss my years as a trailblazer in corporate America and my ascent to the ranks of the global oil industry, where no woman or Black woman had ever gone before. I would rather discuss the honor of being on the cover of *Black Enterprise* magazine's "100 Most Powerful Executives in Corporate America" issue in February 2009 and the benefits of global exposure. I want to take you inside private corporate jets as we fly around the world for high-powered meetings where nothing is too expensive for us. But that wouldn't be the whole story.

If I had not lived my life, I would not believe this story. But I was there. I was the first woman and/or first Black woman to hold high-profile C-level positions in corporate America, from British Petroleum to Burger King. There are so many lessons I want to share, so many dots that need connecting because by doing so, I hope someone reading this book may save themselves years of frustration and hopefully have a more effective path to their own success.

My entire story starts as a little girl born in the Deep South in the late 1950s. My siblings and I were living with my grandparents because our father was dead and our mother was in prison. We have a lot to talk about.

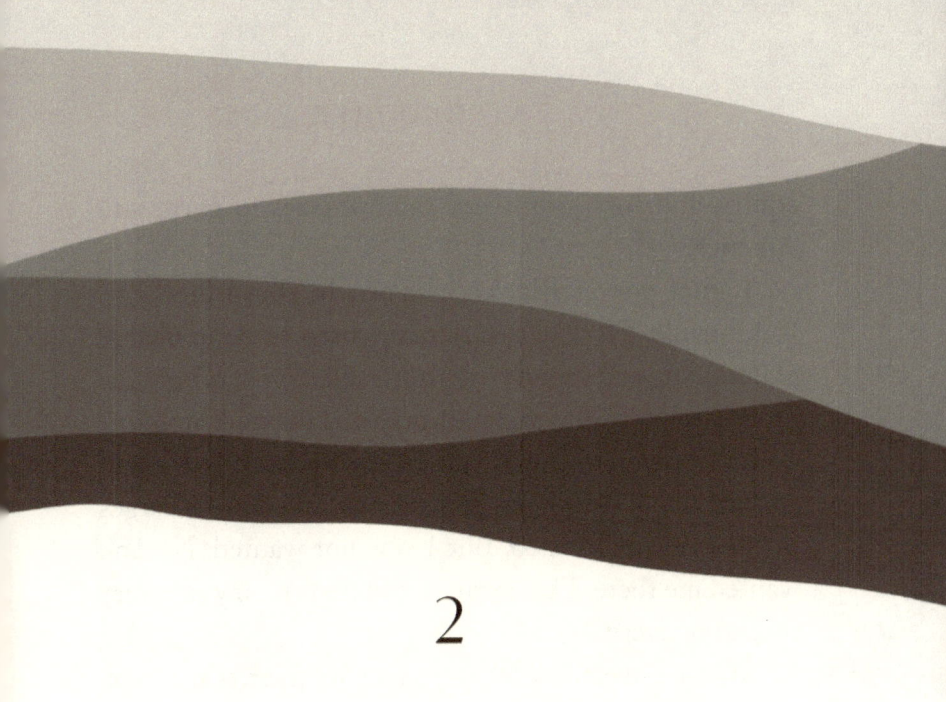

2

A Woman Like Me

After graduating with a BS degree in mechanical engineering in 1979, I entered the oil industry as an engineer in offshore oil and gas exploration and production at Conoco Oil. Then after returning to school and earning my MBA in finance and investment banking in 1986, I went to work at the Standard Oil Company, which shortly thereafter was bought out and became British Petroleum (BP)—and this was decades before diversity, equity, and inclusion were catchphrases in corporate America.

I, that young Black girl born in the projects of Jacksonville, Florida, was not supposed to be in charge of designing and supervising the installation of oil and gas production facilities and routinely making multimillion-dollar decisions—but I was. I flew on helicopters and worked on oil platforms, drilling rigs, and derrick barges in the Gulf of Mexico. But I was not wanted. No one wanted me there. This meant I had to prove myself every second of every day.

Women like me didn't supervise Southern white men, many of them more than double my age. Women like me were not executives responsible for all channels of trade in a major sales division in the second-largest oil company in the world—but I was.

My oil industry years were then followed by executive positions in the restaurant industry, first at Jack in the Box and then at Burger King. I was directly responsible for over two billion dollars in annual sales ($3.8 billion in 2025 dollars) and was jointly responsible for the strategic direction and performance of fourteen billion dollars in annual sales ($27 billion in 2025 dollars) as a Burger King Global Executive Team member.

My time in each industry highlighted one fact: Climbing the corporate ladder is difficult for everyone. But there's something no one tells you. African Americans usually don't have a ladder. We must dig under the wall. While others may have a map to success, we must find a work-around.

While others get feedback and mentorship, we often learn on our own. This, I discovered, is both good and bad.

The bad part is obvious: There is no equity of opportunity. The good part is less obvious, and it is this: By the time an African American earns an executive position, we are often more qualified than our superiors. Our path is more difficult, but those of us who get through are competent at the highest level. We have had to learn the trip wires in corporate America. We see the invisible fences and hear the high-frequency whistles. There is great opportunity once you learn the rules of the game. I personally found that the most helpful course in my MBA program was Organizational Behavior, which covered the how to and the importance of understanding the culture and unwritten rules of an organization. It also covered the critical importance of mentors.

I'm not sure if you can tell already, but I am a very private person. I am more comfortable discussing my professional life than my personal life. But again, that wouldn't be the whole story. Life comes in layers. In and among my unprecedented success in corporate America, there are volatile events as a child; and being diagnosed with spinal stenosis and chronic migraines as an adult, living each day managing intense pain. There are failed relationships and the deaths of my mother, stepfather, five siblings, and my husband of twenty-four years and father to my two children. There was a complete hysterectomy, multiple spine surgeries, and a host of costly lessons learned the hard way.

There is no way to cover it all in this book, but I will

cover a lot. Stay close. My story takes unexpected turns, like the man who molested me dying of HIV, and the day I learned my precious mother killed a man.

I am in my late sixties now (can't believe I said that). Meaning, I am on the short side of my life. The death of my stepson, at almost the same young age as my little brother when he died, was another tug on that thread; things began to unravel. I don't want to waste any more of my precious time, not another second.

I'm having these random thoughts, but there is still another question waiting to be answered. My sister Dee and I had not finished the first sensitive topic when another topic interrupted my thoughts.

"Do you remember Mom on the bathroom floor, crying and screaming?" I asked.

My throat closed again. She whispered her response. "I do remember."

I was referring to a traumatic childhood scene. This was the day my mother said she was running away from the family. She was leaving. My little brother and I found her on the bathroom floor having an emotional breakdown. The scene was just too much. I remember Mom crying, yelling, screaming. My little brother and I stood at the door in shock, watching Pop try his best to console her, and then I heard my mother say something that has stuck with me all these years later.

"I served my time!" she said. "I served my time!"

Even as a kid, I was smart enough to know what that meant, but again, I locked my conclusions safely away in the box. I didn't have the emotional capacity to deal with it. In the end, my dad got Mom to stay. I never asked any more questions about what happened that day, but, looking back now as an adult, I believe Mom was considering suicide. She wasn't threatening to leave the family. She was threatening to leave this world.

Then my sister told me that one day when she was on a train to Washington, DC, a total stranger approached her and started talking as if he was completing an earlier conversation they were having.

"Yeah, you know, that was a terrible thing about your mom. Your grandfather did all he could. He spent every dime he had." She was like, "Huh?" What was he referring to? What did he mean, "Your grandfather did all he could do"? It was shocking for someone you don't know to say something so personal, something so blatant like that. The thread kept pulling, and this incident reminded me of something else.

For several years growing up, four of my siblings and I shared a tiny, single bedroom, which could only squeeze in one set of bunk beds, at my grandparents' house. At times, it was a stressful existence. We had little money and walked on eggshells, meaning, when my grandfather was home, we had to get the heck out of his way. We had to disappear. It was an eggshell life in a house the size of an eggshell.

While living there, I landed a leading part in the school play. I was probably between seven and nine years old. In those days (at least for poor people), clothes and linens that needed to be washed in hot water were boiled outside in a big metal pot. You stirred the clothes with a broom handle. We called it the pot stick. One day, Grandma was in the backyard stirring clothes and I was sitting on the steps of the back porch eating sugar cane from the stalks growing there, when I got up and walked over to her with a request.

"Grandma, I need to get the money for my ballerina outfit for the school play."

"Girl, I don't have any money for that nonsense," she said. "But Grandma, I have to get my costume for the play," I pleaded.

Grandma stopped stirring, looked me dead in the eyes, and said, "You don't have to do anything but stay Black and die."

Those words shocked me, bothered me to my core. You mean, that's all I'm expected to do in life? That's it? Stay Black and die? I was so disappointed. First, I couldn't get my costume because we were poor. Second, and it's hard to explain, but it was kind of a slap in the face. Even though we lived in the racist South, I had never come face-to-face with the fact that my life boiled down to two things—my color and my death.

The weirdest thing about that conversation with my grandma is this: I adored her. She was one of the brightest lights in my life. Grandma could do no wrong. However, her words didn't ring true. I heard what she said, and it broke my heart. But, even as a little girl, I didn't believe her. Something inside of me said I was going to do something with my life. Where that "something inside of me" came from, I don't know. I just knew that I was going to do more than just stay Black and die. I had to do more. Knowing Grandma and her love for me, she was most likely trying to manage my dreams, trying to make sure I understood the kind of world I would be entering one day. She didn't want me to be crushed. In her mind, I needed to know that no matter how excited I might be about an opportunity, it probably wouldn't work out because I'm Black. Looking back, given the trajectory of my professional life, it was probably the best thing Grandma could have told me. It lit a burning fire in me that never went out.

I refused to simply stay Black and die.

My grandfather, the man the stranger on the train was referring to, worked hard, doing the best he could to provide for us. We wore them both out. So, one year, to give my grandparents a break, we were sent to our paternal grandmother's home for three weeks during the summer. I'll never forget it. Our paternal grandparents lived above a grocery store that was more like a corner market where you could buy cookies, pickles, and soft drinks. It was during that summer that I was introduced to a whole different world.

In the house we had just come from, my grandma was very strict with us and made sure we spent a lot of time at church. But my paternal grandmother wasn't very mobile, due to diabetes. So, at our paternal grandparents', we did as the other kids in the neighborhood did and ran the streets with no rules, no supervision. If my life had continued down that path, things for me would have been very different. Only now am I coming to fully grasp that, for the first few years of my life, I didn't have parents. Our grandparents, who were beyond the years of child-rearing, raised us, a point I'll return to later.

The reason we were living with our grandparents in the first place had a lot to do with what my mother said while crying and screaming on that bathroom floor.

When I was about a year old, my mother left us. Not by choice, but by force, and this is another memory I have buried in the box all these years. As a little girl, anytime I wanted to see my mother, I had to go to this facility. I had no idea what it was, but it was loud, and someone had to let us in and let us out. We would sit on the metal bench and play "button, button, who's got the button?" while waiting to see Mom.

This is when my siblings and I lived with our grandparents. Grandma gave me my moral foundation. I learned my belief system from her, a system that has stayed with me all these years. You'll hear me refer to my belief system often because it is my core. It took me all over the world, and Grandma—my mother's mother—gave it to me. The foundation of her teaching was simple: Don't lie, cheat, steal, or kill, and treat others as you want to be treated. She taught me to always tell the truth and never compromise my integrity. That was my foundation, so it's no wonder I would one day have to be honest about everything. I was raised that way.

After about five and a half years, Mom came home and later married my stepfather. Life was better. They built us a house. Three girls slept in one bedroom, three boys in another. The house was actually very nice for a Black family in the South. Compared with our previous home, we were entering the middle class. Mom loved it, and I had a sense of home.

As I got a little older, I noticed things I hadn't noticed before. Many women, including family and friends of the family, were suffering from emotional and physical abuse. I can remember holding on to my mother's leg as a little girl during one violent incident. The details are cloudy, but I remember we were by the kitchen stove, as someone was screaming and fighting. In most cases, the women stayed in these toxic relationships because of the man's money. They couldn't earn enough to provide for themselves and their kids. So, staying with their abusers was how they tried to ensure that their children would have food and shelter.

At a tender age, I decided I didn't ever want to be in that situation. I never wanted to subject myself to certain abusive behaviors simply because I couldn't take care of myself. So, I was motivated at a much younger age than the average person. I did not want to live the life I had witnessed around me. The interesting thing is, my decision to be self-sufficient became a double-edged sword. For a woman, self-sufficiency has its own set of unique problems in our personal relationships with men. By the time I was twenty-two, I was married, was the chief breadwinner, and was now facing all the challenging dynamics this would present throughout our marriage, especially decades ago.

Dee and I kept talking, kept pulling on that string. Random forgotten memories stretched from adolescence to retirement. The box was open now. Everything was on the table. We went beyond childhood, into high school, into my college days on the campus of Tuskegee University, where Tuskegee's own Lionel Richie and the Commodores would perform in the university's gym.

Then we talked about my relationship with my stepfather. In my eyes, he was a saint walking this earth. I mean, what man with three children marries a woman with six children and works himself to death taking care of them? We had a good father-daughter relationship. But, even then, life is complicated, and my sunshine is another person's rain.

We can all relate to struggles of some sort. Whether you grow up as a young Black kid in the inner city or grow up in luxury in the finest communities, we all have weight we carry because of something we know that no one else knows. We all have something in the box.

In my case, one of the things in the box gave me super drive and purpose. I refused to just stay Black and die.

3

Heavenly Protection

P overty is a heck of a drug. When you grow up around it, you notice how certain people are committed to maintaining their negative economic condition, just like others are committed to maintaining their cocaine habit. Meaning, their decisions keep them poor.

In such an environment, you can start to believe you are your surroundings. You can believe illegal activity is your only way out. I have seen this firsthand and can tell you this is true. But again, that's only half the story. Yes, poverty produces failure and death, but did you know it also produces greatness and life?

It is complicated because depending on the individual, poverty can be the best or worst thing to ever happen to you. Many of my family and childhood friends suffered negatively from being poor. Many succumbed to illicit drugs, alcohol, low self-esteem, and a host of other negative outcomes. Poverty makes you think there is no hope.

I say all of this for you to appreciate the environment in which certain violent acts took place around me. I am a big believer in personal responsibility and discipline. The accomplishments in my life, second to the grace of God, have happened because I took ownership for my actions, and I did what needed to be done in order to have a better existence. I could have easily gone to the right or to the left, but I chose to stay centered. That said, certain environments do agitate and nearly guarantee certain behaviors.

Big cities like Detroit, New York, and Chicago are known for the challenges its poor residents face day to day, but other than scale, the vices in these cities are no different from the vices you find in smaller cities. I would go even further and say that the small-mindedness found in lesser-known towns is a far more damaging vice than many of the sins found in larger cities. You can enter a treatment center for your drug addiction, but there is no treatment center for your addiction to small thinking.

Jacksonville is the northernmost city on the east coast of Florida. Its counties abut southern Georgia, with whom it shares the same type of culture. Most of the Black residents in Jacksonville were poor when I was growing up. A quick search through the 1970 Bureau of the Census published by the US Department of Commerce reminded me that when I was only thirteen years old, nearly 70 percent of all Black families in my city lived near or below the poverty line. Even those above the poverty line lived in low-income areas. My family was one of them.

Many of my childhood friends and classmates are dead. This is not new to many of you reading this, as you can say the same about your childhood friends. This reality among African Americans is very common. But still, that is only half of our story.

What is uncommon is elevating the profile of individuals who were born in these tough environments, yet who still achieved what society says is beyond their reach.

The story of Black families across the width and breadth of this country is a nuanced one. Our communities are running over with genius; however, if you don't believe an area has diamonds, why would you buy the excavation equipment and hire the appropriate personnel to dig the diamonds out of the ground? You wouldn't. To use an example I am familiar with, you only drill for oil in places you believe have oil.

There are such low expectations placed on our communities as a whole that the only skill set most of the world identifies with people of color is our physical talent in the area of sports. I would offer that these physical gifts are actually the least of what we have to offer. I wasn't the only smart kid in my neighborhood; far from it. I wasn't the only girl talented with understanding math, science, and physics. I was just one of the ones who got out.

In chapter one, I presented a small taste of life living with my grandmother, but to fully understand her, and the role she played in my personal and professional life, I must back up just a bit and fill in a few gaps.

My grandmother's name was Gladys. I am named after her. Grandma took me into her hands, like a piece of clay, and molded me during the first seven years of my life. She taught me life principles, and then poured concrete on them. Certain things were huge—like cleanliness is next to godliness. To this day, I'm still a clean freak because of it. In her eyes, you could be poor and have one dress, one outfit in life, but it was to be clean at all times. Sew up the holes. You were going to look neat and perfect. It didn't matter if the clothes were hand-me downs, you were to keep yourself presentable. No questions asked.

During my childhood, Grandma was sweet, but angry, and understandably so. Think about it: Six children were basically forced upon her to raise in her older years. I'll explain how that happened in a moment. Sometimes, her frustrations got the best of her and would run over into her discipline of us. Many Black families can remember their parents grabbing a switch from a nearby tree to provide a quick correction for an act of disobedience. Well, one day Grandma was so upset that she just grabbed the nearest thing at hand, which happened to be a cowboy boot. Oh my God! I'll never forget it. That beating would make for a great country song. But Grandma was also the one who set a fire in me to be great.

I was always a smart kid. But I talked a lot, too much in fact. When I came home with my first-grade report card, I had wonderful grades, but I had a C in conduct. There was a note written next to this grade. The note said, "Gladys talks too much in class."

My grandmother beat the living crap out of me! She lost it. In her mind, everybody might not be a genius, but damn it, you should know how to behave!

There is a joke in my family about this incident. Since the day I got that correcting from Grandma, since the first grade on, I brought home straight A's. She literally beat me into success. And of course, I kind of say this jokingly because there were other elements in my life that taught me valuable lessons early on, but that beating in the first grade, for getting a C in conduct, seemed to jump-start me, like the Energizer Bunny.

There was another reason I made good grades. I had a big family and was next to the youngest. My family was trying to help send all of us kids to college. But I knew there wouldn't be enough money left by the time they got to me. My scholastic achievement was the only thing that gave me a remote chance of an education. My mother didn't get to finish high school. She wanted so much more for her children. I saw an academic scholarship as my path to making that happen for me. I wasn't an athlete. I was a cheerleader, but no one was giving out cheerleading scholarships. In order to make a life, I had to make the grades.

I was also very active in school activities and held many leadership positions. But due to financial strains, neither my siblings nor I had a car, and my parents were not available to drive me to and from my activities. I walked or took the city bus to go to practices and other extracurricular activities. My mom was a great seamstress and would make my uniforms and outfits for special events. I also learned to sew rather well and made clothes for myself.

My parents worked very hard. They even had second jobs cleaning Dairy Queens at night. Sometimes, I was allowed to come along and help. But despite them doing the best they could, they suffered with the disappointment of not being able to do more. I can remember working hard as a student leader to help organize the senior class trip to the Bahamas. However, I didn't go on the trip because my parents couldn't afford it. I understood and didn't blame my parents. But they felt so awful about me missing the trip. Seeing how disappointed they were for what they saw as letting their child down was another reminder that I wanted to be financially secure when I became an adult. I didn't want to go through that kind of guilt as a parent, and I didn't want my children to have to deal with these types of disappointments either.

⸻

Okay, before I get back to why I was being raised by my grandmother, let me first say this.

My mother loved her children with all her heart, and I loved my mother dearly. She was the strongest person

I have known. When she returned home, she was the backbone and glue of the family. She survived the loss of four children, her husband, and both of her siblings (all dying at young ages). Three of her children and her husband died in her arms. But instead of giving up, she grew stronger and closer to God throughout these difficult times. She became a great source of spiritual strength and leadership for so many in her life. When she died, at the age of seventy-two, her dying wish and concern was to be sure I was draped in faith and the love of God. Mom, you can rest in peace.

For the answer about my mother's absence, I had to call my big sister Dee again. She is now the matriarch of our family.

I admitted to her that I knew deep down inside that something bad had happened, but that I guess I had just preferred not to have to face the disturbing details. I preferred to live in the world that my family wanted for me, a world where I didn't have to know.

So I asked Dee, "Do you know what happened?"

She said, "Yes. But it's not pretty."

Our mother was a beautiful woman and was in a relationship with a jealous and abusive boyfriend. If any other man showed interest in my mother, he would go into a rage. If a man flirted with my mom, he would beat my mother up as a result. He would essentially beat my mother because she was pretty. They went out to a club one night and another man tried to flirt with my mother. Her boyfriend went ballistic, blamed her, and said he was going to kill her.

Things continued to escalate, and she ended up shooting him that night. She was sent to prison for manslaughter.

Many years later, after the stranger confronted my sister on the train, Mom spoke to my sister about the incident. She assured her that she had no choice that night. It was either she killed him or she wouldn't be here.

I quietly thought of the prayer of serenity. This information about my mother qualified as something I could not change. I wondered whether she would have been taken away from us had the incident happened after the civil rights movements of the 1960s and '70s. That was a time when women and people of color had slightly greater protections against domestic violence and a greater voice against injustice in general. Thinking back, this is probably why my grandmother was so adamant about proper behavior at all times. Simply put, there was no room for error for a Black girl in my world.

It is interesting how all of this happened during my early years. In many ways, it seems I was protected either by ignorance or just because I wasn't around. Almost as if God kept me right on the outside of trouble because He had a mission for me. It may seem crazy, but I've always felt that I had a blessing on my life—that God was always looking out for me, protecting me. Too much has happened that could have destroyed me. If it weren't for the grace of God, I could be living under a bridge right now.

My feeling of heavenly protection started when I was nine years old. I was sitting alone in church one Sunday because Pop was singing in the choir, and when they opened the doors to the church, meaning, when the pastor invited people to give their life to Christ and to be baptized, I stood up and gave mine. I got up, walked to the front of the church, and joined.

The minister came over to me and asked why I had made this decision, and my answer was, "I love Jesus and want to give my life to Christ."

That is when I felt a certain protection from heaven that continues till this day. Little did I know how much I was going to need it. Little did I know.

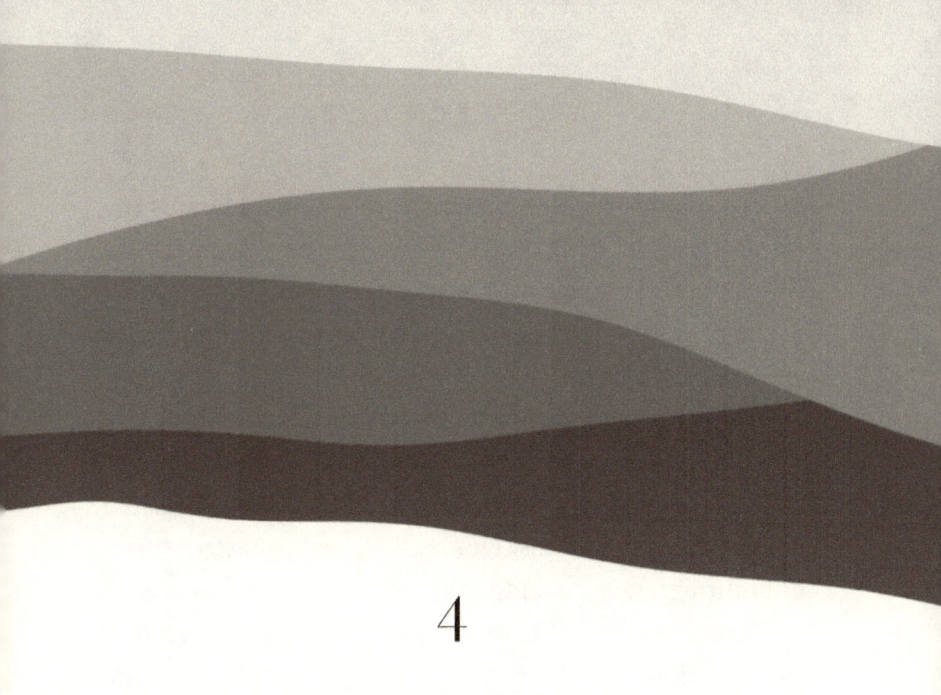

4

A Higher Platform

"I am Shirley Chisholm."

Everything is still. My words echo throughout the auditorium, bouncing from wall to wall for what seems like an eternity. Slowly, I look up from my notes—the place is packed. Everyone is looking directly into the center of my eyes. I am nervous, but for some reason, I love it.

The pressure doesn't bother me at all. I stand there, taller than my height. I am so proud. My eyes move right to left, briefly stopping on the faces I know. There is my classmate right there, and my teacher, the principal is in the back, and the girls I cheer with at our games are all in the front row. No one moves. No one says a word. I have everyone's attention.

I look the part too. My socks are striped knee-highs, red, white, and blue. I pair them with a pleated navy-blue skirt, a freshly ironed white blouse, and a red double-breasted blazer with gold buttons. This is 1972. I am a fourteen-year-old ninth grader speaking in front of the school assembly.

Every teacher and every student have this interesting look on their faces. I can only imagine what they were thinking. First, nowhere in society is a Black woman up front leading anything. Nowhere in society does a Black woman command everyone to stop what they're doing and listen. Generally, we sit at the very bottom of every meaningful list. But on this day, I represent a Black woman who dares to run for the presidency of the United States. She dares to do something she knows will not end in success—that is, if you believe success is only defined by winning. "I am Shirley Chisholm." I can still hear myself saying those words today.

On that day, over fifty years ago, I wrote and gave a campaign speech about Ms. Chisholm's plans to be the leader of the free world. For those few minutes, I was her. It took decades, but eventually the words I spoke that day became reality. It took decades, but my life would strangely begin to transform into hers, not in the area of electoral politics, but in the halls of corporate power. In boardrooms where no Black woman has entered other than to collect plates and silverware. I was destined to one day break the gender and racial barrier at some of the most powerful corporations on earth.

For context, Shirley Anita St. Hill Chisholm was the first African American woman in Congress (1968) and the first woman and African American to seek the nomination for president of the United States from one of the two major political parties (1972). Her motto and title of her autobiography—*Unbought and Unbossed*—illustrates her outspoken advocacy for women and minorities during her seven terms in the US House of Representatives. I was proud to associate myself with such a woman. I identified with her. She was bold, smart, articulate, and brave. She did not cave under pressure, especially the pressure of doubt from those who desired to maintain the status quo. She represented everything I wanted to be, even as a young girl.

I'll never forget running home after school to tell my parents how great my speech went that day in 1972. I detailed everything. I told them that by the time I finished, the people who were staring at the beginning were the same people clapping and cheering at the end. The speech was a moment of clarity for me. A moment that convinced me that maybe, just maybe, I could do something big with my life, just as Ms. Chisholm had done with hers. My spirit leaped for joy. This was a foreshadowing of things to come. Leadership was in my bones. It seemed no matter what group or organization I was in, I ended up being the leader. I was drafted, maybe because I simply could not stand around and watch inefficiency or incompetence. I would speak up, and for many, speaking up means placing your hat in the ring to lead the changes you suggest need to be made.

I learned a lesson about leadership at a young age after giving that political speech. Leadership doesn't mean what you lead will actually work. It really means that if you lead with integrity, hard work, and with an open heart and mind for constructive criticism, you raise the floor. Those coming behind you now have a platform, a higher platform of excellence upon which they can lead even greater than you could. In that way, leadership is not being the star, but enabling others to become stars after you.

Chisholm didn't win the presidential election of 1972, but by simply trying, by getting in the fight, she created an unforgettable example of what it takes to move the needle in society. Looking back, her campaign was probably the first time I realized you don't have to win to win. You win by wrestling your fear to the ground and getting into the race. Before her death in 2005, Chisholm was asked how she wanted to be remembered. She said, "I want to be remembered as a woman who dared to be a catalyst of change." Daring to be a catalyst of change means your unselfishness prepared the way so those coming behind you would have a greater chance at success than you did. Now, think about what happened to those who came behind her.

Millions of college students today were just kids when President Barack Obama was elected. How they view color, race, and career possibilities is vastly different than those of us who grew up in the 1960s and '70s. It is complicated, because while so much has changed, so much has not. The challenge for young professionals today is to know the difference between the two.

I imagine if I were navigating the corporate world today, things would be different. If I were just graduating college and seeking to enter into the workforce, what would be my greatest challenge? It's an interesting thought experiment because the rules today have changed a bit. Corporate America is still an animal, but not the animal it was in the 1980s.

This animal today may have lost a step. It has fewer racist and sexist fangs. This point should not be overlooked, because being successful in corporate America is largely a psychological game. The psychological game goes something like this: Keep talented people unaware of their true talent. If you don't believe you belong, you won't. If you doubt yourself, everyone around you will do the same. President Obama told an entire generation, "You belong in the White House." Think about that.

When I was coming up, there was no public example of someone like me who had reached the nation's highest office. There were no Black folk in politics or corporate leadership calling the shots. Such an idea was unheard of. The only place you could find us was running, jumping, and catching on the sports field. It is really difficult to convince others you can do a certain thing when no one on the planet who looks like you has done what you claim you can do. Maybe this is why, as a child, my mind gravitated toward the big screen where people pretended to have positions and respect that they didn't have in real life. These were the years when I wanted to become an actor. I wanted to be great, if only in my mind.

I would sit at home on weekends staring into our black-and-white television watching actors like Diahann Carroll and Sidney Poitier. I was spellbound by their gifts, but when I think about it now, it wasn't just their gifts that made me so interested. It was seeing the other side of Black culture that I never saw highlighted on American television.

When you grow up poor, you notice that while many Black households are economically poor, just as many are intellectually and creatively rich. You notice that there is a big difference between the Black people you know and the ones the media puts on television. There are potential doctors, lawyers, engineers, and architects in our communities that either never had an opportunity to go to school, or made decisions that took them down a negative path. You can find everything in our communities, from the smartest, most elegant people you will ever meet, to those who have less than noble agendas. But we most often see the latter in the media. However, when I watched certain movies, like *Guess Who's Coming to Dinner?*, I saw the best of who we are.

In Diahann Carroll, I saw sophistication, beauty, elegance, and grace. In Poitier, I saw strength, intellect, and pride. In other words, in my mind, if acting was the job that allowed me to be these things, then sign me up!

The little I learned about acting in middle and high school also gave me insight into the world I would occupy one day. Actors have to know how to convincingly become someone they are not, yet do it honestly. This seems to be contradictory. How does one become something they aren't and remain honest? Black folk do it every day.

After college and graduate school, I landed in many situations where I needed the kind of acting skills seen in Hollywood. I found myself staying true to what Grandma taught me concerning integrity, while at the same time taking on a language and a comportment that, at times, made me feel like I was acting in a well-funded movie.

Walk into a room full of white executives from Ivy League schools, who come from wealth, and doing this as a Black woman from Jacksonville, Florida, you can find yourself changing how you talk, move, and smile. You find yourself acting the role of a well-behaved subordinate who knows how to make everyone around her feel comfortable. But you also notice how no one else has taken on that same burden to make you feel comfortable.

My voice was controlled, my movements were fluid. I dressed the part. I knew the exact distance from which I should shake the hand of a man, and then of his wife. What eye contact to make, and for how long. When to look away, and where to look once I did. I knew when to laugh at jokes that were not funny. I became a great actor because corporate America is the biggest movie set on earth. However, I do believe you can do all of this acting from a place of honesty. Life comes in layers. Let me explain.

Ever watch a movie where the actor didn't convince you he was really a villain? Something about the way he pulled his gun, perhaps, made you feel the whole scene was fake. Business works the same way. While you must learn the language, you cannot pretend to have a soul if you don't have one. You cannot pretend to care when you don't. In other words, you can say all the right lines, but you can never convince others that you have a heart if you don't, and this is where I found my secret sauce.

If you take care of your people, you will always win, and by your people I'm talking about everyone in your workforce, those on every level and in every role, including the janitors and cleaning ladies. I'm talking about hourlies, professionals, managers, executives, those in the mail room, and the receptionists who answer the phones. When you care about everyone, including those in the lowest ranks of your organization, something odd happens. You are given a certain authority that money can't buy. And right there is where acting stops and honesty starts. Treating people with dignity gives you human capital, which is the most valuable commodity on earth. I didn't learn that in graduate school. I learned that from Grandma. I learned that from my mother.

5

Victim and Benefactor

Childhood is like a circus: Look closely and you can find almost anything. This is why so many of us prefer, still today, not to look too closely. It is complicated—layered—because right when we locate incredibly good experiences, we can find they live right next door to experiences that are not so good. One thing is for sure: As children, exposure makes us all a victim and a benefactor. You cannot separate the two. As it relates to women, many of us learn at a very young age to keep our mouths shut and behave. We are rewarded for behaving, but we rarely make a mark if we do. I wanted to make a mark, and so things got interesting; more on that later.

As children, what we see and what we hear during our development stages has more to do with shaping our perspective than many of us are comfortable admitting. Exposure shapes our perspective; our perspective shapes our future.

This very book you are reading is an outgrowth of how small my world was while I was growing up, and how much it expanded once I left home. My perspective changed. In fact, how I classify the socioeconomic condition of my family while living in Jacksonville is interesting. I've had time to reconsider, in conversations with Dee, whether we were poor or middle class, because as you know, poverty is relative.

The relativity and the effects of poverty are a book all unto themselves. By some estimates, the average Black family has one-tenth the wealth of the average white family, so even the term "middle class" is biased, because whose middle are we referring to?

What I do know is, my mother's family was a solidly middle-class Black family (by Black middle-class standards). My grandfather had a good job with the railroad. I believe he retired from there after thirty years of service. My grandmother worked downtown at a jewelry store, behind the scenes with stuff like gift wrapping, and so on. My grandparents were planning to send all three of their daughters to college. The oldest daughter had already started. Then my grandparents' financial condition became much worse, as I mentioned in earlier chapters, after they spent their financial means on legal help for my mother and took in all six of us kids to raise. Consequently, the oldest daughter had to drop out of college, something I recently found out. Growing up, I would always hear that my aunt was the first one in the family to go to college. I had assumed that she finished her degree and graduated. But now I know that was not true and that she didn't get to finish because of financial reasons. Truth is the greatest exposure of all. That said, something else must be added. Even with exposure, we also need guidance.

For me, Momma, Grandma, siblings, and a host of family and friends represent my first guidance counselors. They guided me in positive ways. Directly or indirectly, I learned what was valuable, what was safe, and what was dangerous. However, at some point I found myself at a crossroads. I had to learn to separate the good people I loved from whatever bad information they may have given me.

I say that because childhood is like those clay molds that we played with in arts and crafts somewhere around the second or third grade. We come here empty, and then someone, hopefully someone who has our best interest at heart, pours a belief system into us. This belief system hardens like concrete. Our character and personality take shape and form. But sometimes we forget that people can only pour into us what has been poured into them.

We wake up one day and begin to question whether the belief system that shaped us should remain with us forever. But even when we decide we believe differently than our family and friends, it can take a lifetime to break out of the concrete mold, or at least to scrape the edges off to fit the life we desire for ourselves. It can take a lifetime to recognize how certain beliefs have helped or harmed us. It can take a lifetime to discover if what was presented to us as truth is actually true.

When I say *belief*, I am not simply referring to morals like don't lie, cheat, or steal. A belief system not only teaches us morality, but how to manage the immoral acts of others. I should say that again. Our belief system not only teaches us morality, but how to manage the immoral acts of others. Our belief system tells us when to speak and when to keep quiet. Belief systems have kept millions of predators out of prison because somewhere, early on, a child or an adult was taught to keep quiet about anything that would embarrass others or cause physical or emotional harm, even when physical or emotional harm was done to us by the very person we are protecting. We are victims and benefactors.

Exposure, belief, and guidance are so powerful that you would be hard-pressed to find a successful person who did not have at least one person tell them they would be successful one day. And it would be just as difficult to find someone who quit on their dreams who had not been encouraged to quit. And if you're looking for any evidence of this, consider me.

I have benefitted so much from family, friends, and teachers who believed in me. But I also learned a lot about keeping my mouth shut. Certain looks and gestures can be as clear as a spoken command. I could read the tea leaves. Early on, I knew how to move about with a smile on my face so others could save face. It was a skill that allowed me to be victimized during one stage of my life, but it also contributed to my success later in life. Life comes in layers, and belief is complicated. It is never all good or all bad. This conversation brings back some interesting high school moments.

First, let me tell you a bit of background about my high school. If you are a Black person from Jacksonville and you ever run into another Black person from Jacksonville, one question is sure to be asked: Ribault or Raines? Those were the two high schools most of the Black students in Jacksonville attended. They are located very close to each other, and the students are friends, neighbors, and archrivals in sports. The boundary lines between the two school districts shifted throughout the years. My own household was split down the middle between Raines and Ribault graduates.

Both of these schools have an interesting racial background. In 1964, with an increase in Jacksonville's African American population, Duval County School Board decided to send African American students to Jean Ribault High School, but the all-white faculty and students rejected the idea. The school board then decided to build a new facility, costing two million dollars. That school's doors opened in 1965, and it was later named William Marion Raines High School. It was the first school in Duval County to achieve accreditation and was the very best that Jacksonville had to offer Black students.

However, Jacksonville was still not appropriately meeting the desegregation laws. So, in 1971, it was decided to pair Ribault and Raines to achieve integration goals. They both would have grades ten through twelve and would split the African American population. It was anticipated that the Black enrollment at Raines would be 59 percent and Ribault would be 57 percent. Interestingly, I was a seventh grader that year and was sent to Ribault Junior High School, where I lived through very violent race riots at school because of integration. I can still remember having to hide under desks to seek protection from other desks that were being thrown at us by white students.

Both Raines and Ribault High Schools have gone through many cycles since I graduated fifty years ago. But the question—Raines or Ribault—still remains. I was just asked that again recently. To which I proudly replied, Raines.

Actually, I was not supposed to go to Raines because we lived just outside the current school district line. But Raines High was the better academic school at that time (as well as the top athletic school). I strongly wanted to attend Raines, and my mom wanted me to get the best education. So, she went through the necessary steps to get me transferred to Raines.

We had excellent, dedicated teachers. They held students to the highest of academic standards. We had organizations, like the Ladies of Raines and the Rainesmen Club, that were aimed at helping us achieve excellence in everything we did. Our teachers wanted us to go beyond the lives we had in our communities. They strove to expose us to a higher level of thinking.

Recently as I was recalling these memories, the phone rang.

It was my sister Dee.

"How are you, girl?" she asked.

"I'm good, just sitting here thinking about the old days again. Some stuff I haven't thought about in years."

"Still reminiscing, huh?" Dee asked.

"Yeah, our call the other day opened a door. Now I'm remembering things I never knew I knew.

"So, do you remember Mr. K?" I asked. Without giving Dee a chance to answer, I gave his description.

"Mr. K was one of my teachers. He was a tall man and he wore one of those long, hippie-like ponytails. Really nice, smart guy. The kids liked him because he was considered hip. You know how sometimes you can sense that someone else has feelings for you? I thought Mr. K had a crush on me. Even though I was just a teenager—I know, I know, sounds laughable because Mr. K was never inappropriate toward me, until he was."

"Remind me what happened," Dee asked.

"He used to drive a van. One of those hippie vans that had curtains in it. You know? People don't really drive those anymore; you have to pull up a movie from the '70s to see one. Anyway, he gave me a ride home from school one day; not just me, though. It was a group of us students in the van. He dropped me off and of course that's when he found out where we lived. And then, on another occasion, out of the blue one day, I looked outside and Mr. K was in our driveway. I went outside to the van and asked what he was doing there. I don't remember the conversation, but I know we were chatting at the van. He was inside at first, and I was standing outside the driver window. Then he got out. It just felt like something was off. And then the thought hit me, Mr. K is flirting with me."

"Okay, then what happened?" Dee asked impatiently.

"I just remember when it was time to go, you know when nothing else was really left to be said. It was sort of like when somebody leans in like they're going to give you a hug?"

"Yesss," Dee said slowly.

"Well, that was when he tried to kiss me. I moved, turned my face, and pretended like I didn't realize what he had attempted. Things were weird in class after that, but I dealt with it."

"Why don't I know this? Why is this the first time I ever heard about this?" Dee asked.

"You were in college," I responded. "I kept all of this to myself and of course never told the family."

"I don't get it," Dee said.

"Oh, you get it. I didn't want Pop or our brothers to end up in jail for assaulting my teacher. So, I figured it was best to keep my mouth shut, play dumb, and graduate from high school."

"Got it. I don't really agree, but I understand," Dee said.

"For me, thinking about Mr. K and what happened was not so much about him, but really about how I carried this approach throughout my life, long after high school. I was often placed in positions where it was best to play dumb and pretend something never happened.

"Most professional women have to play dumb on a consistent basis. It's almost a virtue. We can't really see what we see or hear what we hear. I would like to think that today things are changing a bit with the #MeToo movement and the like. But still, to keep something bigger from happening, sometimes it's best to play dumb. It is the classic victim protecting the predator syndrome, and it starts in childhood. It's crazy when you think about it. Men hate being rejected, even if they were rejected from doing the wrong thing. Even if they were rejected from abusing you. If you can somehow let the guy feel he hasn't been blatantly disgraced, there is less hostility and potentially less retaliation."

I went on. "Rejection is really the issue, but again, this sounds crazy because the person we should be talking about is the woman who is being violated, or potentially violated. The entire thing is convoluted. Guess that's really why I never exposed Mr. K. I was saving his face even though he tried to kiss mine."

I could tell Dee was trying to process all that I had just told her. She said, "We learn how to deal with problems by first seeing how others deal with their problems. The reason why you didn't say anything about Mr. K, or your molestations years before, is because you weren't given the space to be honest about another person's dishonesty or inappropriate actions. In our community, the Black community, and I suspect in others as well, you can learn fifty years later that your cousin is really your sister or that who you call auntie was really your stepmother. Secrets run deep. There are some things you just don't talk about. You should, I should, but we don't."

My sister continued. "Women are taught to hide. You learn as a child that if you speak, the blame is probably going to find its way back to you somehow. What did you have on? You know the questions. What I'm saying is that we learn as children everything we do as adults. The only difference is, our adult actions are a more sophisticated form of our childhood teachings.

"So, when you became a professional working with a multibillion-dollar company and sexual harassment or inappropriate behavior came your way, the sophisticated adult Gladys didn't handle the problem; Gladys the child did. You are making me think of my own experiences. What did I hide? What did I see that I didn't see? What was said that I pretended I didn't hear?"

"Wow, Dee," I said.

"I know, Gladys. You're opening up a can of worms. In fact, at this point, the worms are snakes. The problems we have today are the problems we have always had. Nothing is new, just more nuanced, more refined. But there are two sides to our childhood. Think about it this way. You were brilliant at ten. Guess what? Today at sixty-seven, you still are. Nothing really changes. It's just that now you have a license for your intellect. Before college, before graduate school, you didn't have an official license to be smart. College and university didn't create you, they just stamped you with their seal of approval. So, it's really deep when you think about it." She paused, then said, "I have a question. Why did you go to Tuskegee instead of Harvard or some other school?"

Since I had been the class valedictorian and a Silver Viking award winner, among many other achievements, the school counselors and key teachers took a high interest in providing me guidance for my college plans. I had always been on the advanced college track program and performed well in the sciences and math, like physics, chemistry, calculus, and so on. There seemed to be general consensus among them that I should go into engineering because I had the aptitude to be an engineer, and it was a field in high demand that paid very well. There also seemed to be the prevailing thought among them that as a Black student, I should attend a Black college of excellence and not miss out on what was referred to as the Black college experience.

In addition, I had a biology teacher who became an advocate for me. I believe his sister had graduated as valedictorian of Raines High a year or two before me, and had taken advanced, college-track courses like I did. She then went to college to study engineering or some other science and technology field, and he felt that her future was looking great. So he pushed for me to follow the same path. He told me it was possible.

The counselors and other teachers agreed. Never mind that at that point, I still didn't really know what an engineer was. I never knew one, had never met one. I had heard of Tuskegee because of its rich history—the Tuskegee Airmen, George Washington Carver, Booker T. Washington, and others. In the end, I went and did exactly what my teachers and counselors suggested I do. I did have options, including scholarships to Vanderbilt and other universities, but I followed the advice of my teachers. No one mentioned I should try to get into an Ivy League school. Those institutions weren't even on my radar. To be honest, I'm not sure I even knew the term "Ivy League" at that point. Hard as I try, I don't remember the option even being presented to me (and remember I didn't have Google and the internet back then).

So I went to the place that had the most momentum in my life. If the momentum had been for Cornell or Princeton, I probably would have gone there.

"So, tell me," Dee said, "if you had to do it all over again, would you have taken the same Black college pathway or gone to another institution? Do you think it's more important to go to a school where people see you? You know what I mean? People see you; people support you; you have a shared background. Or is it more important to go to a school that has a global reputation for being the Ivy League type? If you would have gone to one of the other schools, do you think people would have seen you and thought you got there through some government program, but not because of your intellect?"

After a long pause, I replied, "Those are a lot of tough questions and there are no crystal balls. Graduating from an Ivy League school absolutely would have made my acceptance in corporate America easier, and therefore would have made climbing the corporate ladder easier and faster. But going to Tuskegee provided me the opportunity to be a part of one of the greatest legacies in Black history. It gave me such pride to be part of what was a wonderful and fun experience, which also allowed me to develop vast leadership skills, along with providing me an excellent academic education. So, it would still be a tough call for me.

"But," I continued, "if I had gone to an Ivy League school, I absolutely would not have been concerned about people not seeing me, or viewing me as someone who hadn't earned my spot based on merit. Simply because of who I am. I would have made them see me no matter where I went. I would have made my presence known and earned the respect of others. Doesn't matter what school it was, by the time I left, they would have known I was one of the best students there. I don't sit back and wait for things to happen; I make them happen. I knew every professor's office hours and kept their schedules close. If I didn't understand something, I was at the door and not afraid to ask questions."

But what I didn't know was getting someone to open a corporate door would be much different than the doors at college.

6

Courage

We were still in the taxi, moving at a snail's pace, as if the driver could sense my amazement and was allowing time for me to take it in. This was THE Tuskegee Institute. I noticed there were only a few people on the Alabama campus. Things were rather sparse. I turned around and looked back again at the Booker T. Washington monument. Booker T. is standing upright. He is lifting a veil off the head of a slave who appears to be seated beneath. There is a book in the lap of the slave. There is also a plow. There is an anvil. Right then, the driver slowed to a stop. I could now read the words on the statue.

He lifted the veil of ignorance from his people and pointed the way to progress through education and industry.

This was very moving for me. It was the first day I would step foot on this historic campus. You could feel the energy of possibilities. Something stirred inside me. But I'm getting ahead of myself.

I need to take you back to Jacksonville to the time when I had recently graduated from high school and was full of nerves as I prepared to be a freshman at this legendary institution.

Today, I can recall those past events with calm because I know how things turned out. But back then, I was just a vibrant young woman long on hope and short on resources. I wish I'd had a recipe.

I wish there had been an ingredient list, including tablespoon portions and baking times required to make greatness. The comforting thing about a recipe is, no matter how disorganized the kitchen, no matter how chaotic things look, if you follow the directions, you'll come up with the dish you want to make. There is no such thing for life. However, if you pay close attention, even in chaos, you can feel something stirring. You can feel greatness being made in you.

What I mean by this is, as a child, a teenager, and then a young adult going to college, I always felt like something was being formed of my life. I felt like someone had a hand on me, turning me to the right, then to the left. Moving people and things out of my way so I could take proper shape. I felt like I was headed somewhere great, but I had no idea where that place was or what it was called; I just knew I was meant to do something big.

I felt it when I pretended to be Shirley Chisholm that day in school. I remember realizing my gift for math and science, and how certain things that were difficult for others were not difficult for me. Somehow, I was going to make my mark on the world.

The making of this mark started in earnest once I got to college. Yes, my childhood provided a foundation. But not everyone with a great foundation does something with it. Family and friends groomed me. However, in college I learned something else. I learned to get along with groups of strangers who came from all walks of life. But I also learned how to walk alone and not feel alone. That bears repeating. I learned to walk alone and not feel alone. That lesson started the day I boarded a Florida Amtrak train by myself, in June of 1975, heading to Tuskegee.

There was no planned family trip to help me get settled once I arrived at college or friends with whom I could make memories on the way to my new life. I got on that Amtrak alone, with one blue footlocker with golden buckles, and one torn suitcase. First stop, Montgomery, Alabama. After arriving in Montgomery, I got myself and my luggage to a taxi and paid to be driven the remaining forty miles to campus. I had a lot of time to think on that short yet long taxi ride.

Who would I meet? Would I make the cheerleading squad? Is college like I heard it was? Before I knew it, the taxi driver made a left turn and drove onto the campus of Tuskegee. That's when I saw tall, brick, square-shaped pillars on both sides of the entrance. You know, the kind with the upside-down cone-shaped top and square bricks all the way down. To my right and to my left were rounded sidewalks. There are metal bronze nameplates embedded into both of the pillars, which proudly read *Tuskegee Institute*. Then I saw the famous Booker T. Washington monument. Washington is the founder of Tuskegee. Prior to that very moment, I had only seen this statue in Black history books. And now I was actually here in the flesh.

This was a lot to take in. Tuskegee was made for kids like me. Just entering the campus started making me dream bigger. The manicured grounds, the flowers highlighting the agricultural aspect, and the metalworking anvil representing the technical and manufacturing disciplines. This was another world. The driver turned right and headed toward the main square. That's when I saw the George Washington Carver Museum. And again, I was thinking, *I studied Carver in school.* I had studied his history related to peanut farming, improving the lives and the soil of the rural South; and learned that Henry Ford was his friend, and he used to come sit at Carver's feet and learn. We continued moving and arrived at the square, which was small, but seemed to be the epicenter of campus. The avenue that leads to the square is covered with huge trees that overarch the entire path, providing a cascade of cooling shade.

The administration buildings are mostly red brick and very ornate, with lots of columns—that typical Southern colonial, historical look. All of this is set in the midst of rolling hills and valleys. A huge fountain overflows in the middle of everything, surrounded by concrete benches where students can sit and relax. There are also designated areas for different sororities and fraternities.

It was almost like a movie set where the movie was being made about a secret society of privileged Black kids the world didn't know about. It felt like I was going to be the leading actor. Something was stirring in me. The taxi driver had gone as far as he could take me. He stopped the car and I got out. The driver placed my things on the pavement as if almost to say, *This is your new beginning.* There I am. Gladys from Jacksonville, Florida, standing next to my blue leather footlocker with the gold buckles and my worn suitcase. He drove away. I looked around and saw two frat brothers, from what I would soon learn was Alpha Phi Omega. They looked back at me. It seemed they were just hanging out. One of the guys started talking and moving toward me at the same time.

"Are you new?"

"Yeah," I answered. "I'm trying to check in."

"Well," he said, "I can show you exactly where to go and what to do." He smiled, revealing a small twinkle in his eye. His name was Keith. "My brother will watch your things until we get back," he promised.

Keith proceeded to walk me to the administration building, where I received my dorm assignment and other necessary details. Then I headed to the place where I would live for the next four years. The moment I opened the front door to the dorm, I ran into this young lady. She was tall, dark, beautiful, and had a gorgeous smile. She greeted me with the biggest "Hi! How are you doing?" We became great friends. Both of us later became sweethearts of Alpha Phi Omega fraternity.

Then I met my roommate, Yolanda. She was from Mobile, Alabama. Her family had driven her up by car to Tuskegee and helped her settle in. Yolanda was also a mechanical engineering major. She and I remained roommates until my senior year. It was a whirlwind, meeting students from all over the country and abroad, getting to know professors and figuring out what I was going to do with my life. Over the next couple of days, students rolled in and the campus filled quickly. It was a sight to see. The styles were amazing. So many variations, all with a '70s theme. You would have thought the campus was its own planetary system because circular shapes, better known as afros, seemed to be floating everywhere.

Not just any afros, but every size and shape you can imagine. It was the in thing at the time. It was Black culture, a sign of pride to be able to do something only our hair could do. You could have called us Afro University. As for the girls, they were wearing midriff tops, bell-shaped sleeves, wide-legged bottoms. Oh, and don't forget the platform shoes and leather caps. It was a whole vibe. Guys paired their afros with shirts that had long, pointy collars so sharp you could get a paper cut. Every now and then you'd also catch someone in an evening leisure suit. And speaking of style, my friend Iontha was one of the most consistently put together students of all. Her hair? Always glamorous. Her outfits? High fashion on a daily basis. Her shoes? Impractical for the hills and valleys of campus, but impeccable, nonetheless.

There are a few other unique aspects of Tuskegee, and as I would soon learn, among most historically Black colleges and universities—HBCUs. Our institutions are pledge crazy.

What makes it worse is, our schools are usually small and off in the middle of nowhere by themselves so it's difficult not to go with the flow. As can be expected, Tuskegee University (which back in my day was called Tuskegee Institute) is in a small town. We used to joke that Tuskegee had a population of five thousand, including the chickens and the cows. But it had a tight-knit family feel. Students would gather in the basement of Dorothy Hall near the George Washington Carver Museum and order hamburgers and fries. The only other place near campus where you could eat, other than the cafeteria, was called the "Chicken Coop." And as you would suspect, they served fried chicken covered in this thick, unforgettable seasoning salt.

I say all of that to say, we were pretty much a captive audience. Everyone stayed localized. If we didn't eat on campus, we would have to travel to Auburn (nineteen miles away) or Montgomery (forty miles away) just to get McDonald's or Burger King. And by the way, most of the students did not have cars.

Okay, back to pledging.

You had to pledge everything. I had to pledge cheerleading. Then later when I was inducted into Pi Tau Sigma, the international honor society for mechanical engineers, I had to pledge that too. (Never would I have imagined pledging an honor society.) I later went on to become president of Pi Tau Sigma. (Also, as a side note, back then it was still called an honor fraternity and not an honor society. So, as a female, I was head of a fraternity . . . go figure.) It seemed you had to pledge just to brush your teeth in the morning. It was a lot.

The overindulgence of a pledging culture is one of the reasons that I chose not to pledge a sorority. Given that my priority was my education and academic performance, I didn't feel that I had the time to further invest in pledging. I had too many other obligations already. Plus, I had tons of friends and felt a sense of belonging without it.

After my first year, I had my footing. My routine was set, my relationships were solid. My sophomore year, I was voted Miss Engineering. For the homecoming parade, the engineering students built a Star Wars–themed float for me to ride on. I loved it. Something great was brewing in me.

Also, after completion of my freshman year and having earned straight A's, I was honored as an "Eminent Scholar," which was Tuskegee's highest academic honor. I continued to receive this honor for the rest of my years there. I also continued to develop as a leader. During my four years at Tuskegee, I accumulated the following honors and accomplishments:

- President, Alpha Kappa Mu Honor Society
- President, American Society of Mechanical Engineers (ASME)
- President, Pi Tau Sigma Honorary Engineering Fraternity
- Co-captain, cheerleading squad
- Most Outstanding Mechanical Engineering student
- Selected to Who's Who Among Students in American Universities & Colleges
- Alpha Phi Omega Fraternity Sweetheart
- Miss Engineering
- Graduated summa cum laude (Ranked first in class, with 4.0 grade point average on a 4-point scale)
- Eminent Scholar

A typical day for me was to get up, go to breakfast, then on to an 8 a.m. class; continue my classes throughout the day, go to lunch, and do my homework while studying in between breaks. I would go to cheerleading practice in the evening and go to dinner before going back to my dorm to finish any homework or studying. I did a lot of walking each day. The school of engineering was located on one end of campus, while the other disciplines of study and the cafeteria were in buildings on the opposite side of campus. So, I would always find myself running all the way back and forth across campus a lot. I could have stayed in shape by just going to class.

In between the routine stuff, I would fit in meetings, helping and studying with others, cheering at games (home and away), and going to parties. No doubt, I loved the shared culture of music, dancing, and stepping that made the football games, parties, and campus life so much fun. At the games, the band and cheerleaders constantly worked together with soulful beats and routines to create excitement and involve the fans in the stand. If you can't picture what I'm saying, watch the movie *Drumline*, starring Nick Cannon and others, or probably any other HBCU-focused movie or show. You will also get to see the fun, entertainment, and excitement created by the skillful, rhythmic stepping routines and competitions of fraternities and sororities.

All that said, parties at Tuskegee were usually on the weekend for me because my 8 a.m. classes wouldn't tolerate anything else. Speaking of parties, I do remember one: the Fraternity Ball. I was the frat sweetheart, and one of the brothers got so drunk on Southern Comfort that he puked all over my gold satin gown when he came over to my table to say hello. It was projectile vomit. "Hello," then splat! Quite the memory. My mom was furious. He destroyed the beautiful gown she had made by hand. That's college.

My first summer engineering internship job (at the

end of freshman year) was in Mobile, Alabama, and was the worst job experience I ever had. My college roommate (Yolanda) and I went to work for Alcoa (Aluminum Company of America). There was also a white student named Mary from Duke University on the same internship program with us. I still have a copy of the photo of the three of us working at a drafting table.

I don't recall what they had Mary working on most of the summer. But they had Yolanda and me spend most of our time out in the heat, lugging around heavy surveying equipment and taking survey measurements of the train tracks used to transport the cars of bauxite and alumina powder. Where we worked, the air was filled with dust that covered our clothing and hair. We would go home exhausted and looking like we had been in a flour fight. Plus, my roommate was very petite. She barely weighed ninety-nine pounds. I felt sorry for her and carried the heaviest equipment. This job sucked! And worst of all, it was not utilizing our intellectual abilities or furthering our learning process. I finally went and talked to the boss and told him we needed a change. By the time we were given a different assignment, it was nearly time to return to school.

The summer after my sophomore year, I took an engineering internship job with Conoco at the Gillis Gas Plant, and I lived in Lake Charles, Louisiana. I recall that the bulk of my work centered around a chromatograph project relating to the separation stages of hydrocarbon gases. I also remember that Elvis Presley died while I was working there that summer. A lot of random events happened during my sophomore year. I had dinner in a private dining room with the president of the United States, Gerald Ford, and Tuskegee University President, Dr. Luther Foster, and other officials. During the summer of that same year, when I arrived in Lake Charles for my internship, I was harassed at the hotel where I was supposed to stay until I could move into an apartment. Someone ruined everything in my luggage, covered all my clothes with some liquid oily substance. Someone kept knocking on my room door and running away. They kept ringing the phone in my room and calling me racist names. Things got bad enough that my hiring boss ended up taking me to spend the night at his family's home. I even had to sleep in one of his wife's nightgowns. I did not let this racist treatment deter me. I went on to successfully complete my job that summer. Thinking like an engineer helped me—it was a skill set that I would need in the coming years as I entered uncharted territory.

An engineering mindset not only enables you to objectively analyze and solve problems but can help one manage social offenses. Engineers see everything as a system. They see relationships that aren't apparent to the layperson, they know how to design under constraints, and they understand trade-offs. Adopting an engineering mindset can help reduce stress because engineers tend not to take things too personally. I innately think like an engineer, and I further honed that ability when I studied and worked as an engineer. And even though I went on to earn an MBA in finance and investment banking and then moved on to different career roles and high leadership levels, I still think and always will think like an engineer. When faced with goals and objectives for me and my teams, what I have successfully done my entire career is figure out where we are, where we need to be, and what it's going to take to get us there . . . then make it happen.

What gifts have you been given? What is stirring in you? It is easy to keep these things hidden. It will take courage to show the world your greatness.

7

Welcome to Lake Charles

The excess has been well documented. Working in the oil industry in 1979 was like being a kid in a candy store, and for a while, all the candy was free. This was a time when oversized oil revenues were fueled by rapidly growing markets and discoveries of substantial oil reserves offshore. The wealth surge resulted in higher salaries among executives, skyrocketing stock prices for the largest companies, as well as aggressive hiring of newly minted graduates. And it goes without saying, there were luxurious lifestyles, extravagant corporate events, and marble towers being built as company headquarters—all hallmarks of this era.

Add to this the global events that drove oil prices to record levels. For example, the 1979 Iranian Revolution and Iran-Iraq War caused production levels to decrease; this caused a supply shortage worldwide that pushed oil prices upward. There was a substantial boost for the oil industry in Lake Charles, Louisiana, with its strategic location and established infrastructure serving as an epicenter of production, refining, and distribution activities. All the money moons lined up.

This was the environment I was entering. For me, everything was new. I had just graduated, just gotten married, and was about to start a new job in Lake Charles. Moving there was in no way automatic, however. I had received offers from many different companies. But I was already familiar with Conoco, having done two summer internships with them. However, it was my husband, Michael, who gave them the ultimate advantage. He was from Lake Charles! So, we packed up and headed for the bayou. I soon found out that, just like gumbo, you can find everything there.

I was to work as an engineer in the Oil and Gas Exploration and Production Division. This was June 1979, but at times it felt like 1960. At times it felt like I was carrying the weight and reputation of the entire female gender. I began to feel the pressure of "being first." The first woman in my position, the first Black woman, on and on. Since I had the pressure of first, I decided to be the first to succeed. Winning was my only option.

To fully grasp the challenges of this period in corporate America, one has to think of Lake Charles as being representative of the South at large. In 1979, the South was still recovering from the civil rights movement. Lake Charles, with a Black population of only 20 percent at the time, was in the infancy stage of diversity in all areas of daily life. Corporations like Conoco were trying to figure out how—and if—it was even possible to better incorporate more Black people into their labor forces, not to mention into their leadership. It didn't take long for reality to knock on my door, my bedroom door to be exact. Let me take a step back and explain, because Lake Charles was a smorgasbord of layers. A casserole of the good, the bad, and the shocking. Some days were even hilarious.

I know there's this unwritten rule that you're supposed to tell your life story in the order things happen, but I think skipping ahead a bit and sharing a few experiences relating to the birth and care of my daughter will help you not only understand the world that I was living in, but also the added pressures of life's curveballs. A few years into our marriage, Michael and I got pregnant with our first child. My mother was kind enough to come from Jacksonville to stay with us and help out. To say my pregnancy wasn't easy is like saying the sun is just a little warm. I had morning sickness, false labor pains, prolonged labor, the whole enchilada. The false labor incidents were the worst, seeming like I was "about to have a baby," only to be sent back home and told to get some rest.

Hospital, back home, hospital, back home. This was not only tough on me, but also on Michael because he insisted on coming with me each time. Crazy thing is, he was just very recently out of the hospital after having a major surgery on his stomach and intestines and was barely walking himself. Talk about timing. Also, imagine the very pregnant young wife trying to stay with and take care of her hospitalized husband. It was so stressful that the hospital staff became concerned about me and actually made a bed for me in Michael's room and added checking on me as part of their rounds.

So, I was in my ninth month, and I went to the hospital once again in terrible pain. However, this time I had a different energy. I looked the doctor square in the eyes and said, "Keep me or shoot me." Sounds funny now, but I was so serious. *Take this baby out of me or take me out of this world!* Thankfully, I was in true labor this time. The bad news was, I was too far dilated to have an epidural. I had my baby naturally, and she came out the most beautiful baby on earth! We named her Jeanne-Marie.

Jeanne-Marie was tiny, only five pounds and one-half ounce. She had wrinkled skin like she had been in the pool a bit too long. My doctor said that in hindsight, she had stayed in too long and should have been delivered earlier. He said the delay caused her to lose weight and her skin to wrinkle more. In other words, my baby should have been delivered instead of sending me home, but I digress. While she was perfectly healthy, the small weight was not without its problems. After a couple of months of maternity leave, it was time for me to go back to work, and this is where things got interesting.

We put Jeanne-Marie in day care. She quickly became ill with spinal meningitis, which is an infection of the fluid and membranes around the brain and spinal cord. Once the infection starts, it can spread rapidly through the body. Without treatment, bacterial meningitis can cause brain damage in a matter of hours and can be fatal within twenty-four hours. The really scary part was that they didn't know if the meningitis was caused by a bacterium or a virus. So they did a spinal tap. It would take seventy-two hours to determine the cause of the infection. But if we waited the seventy-two hours before having her treated for bacterial meningitis, she would most likely die. We made a difficult decision and opted to expose our already small, vulnerable child to the medications for bacterial meningitis right away.

Her veins were so tiny they could not get an IV into her the traditional way. They had to perform a cut-down procedure on the vein in her ankle and sew in an IV like they were knitting a blanket. Good news is, it turned out her meningitis was caused by a virus and the treatment was not at all necessary. However, this meningitis episode with my daughter scared the hell out of me and Michael. She would not return to day care. Too many germs, too many other sick children. We needed a more controlled environment.

Now, don't get me wrong. There is nothing wrong with a good day care. They are a must for millions of women who work. But because of her small weight and compromised birth, our daughter needed a different environment. Enter the nanny.

Right when we thought the drama had calmed down, it got a second wind and kept running. The first nanny we hired happened to be an older white lady who lived reasonably close by and seemed really interested in doing the job. She was excellent with Jeanne-Marie and was very reliable. Perfect! However, one morning out of the blue, she didn't show up on time. After waiting for her for a while, we got worried and tried to call. She didn't answer. This was unlike her. We got worried. I contacted her landlord and requested he do a welfare check because something didn't feel right. The landlord went to her apartment and found her sitting on the floor drunk and sobbing uncontrollably. He called us back and gave us an update on what he found. As you can imagine, we were very confused.

She called the next day crying and apologizing for the day before. And then she explained the reason she had been drinking. There had been a big fight with her adult children. Once they found out she was working for a Black family, they came over and threatened her. They told her she was embarrassing the family.

How could you take care of a nigger baby? her kids asked.

They threatened to have her institutionalized if she didn't quit. She said she told them she was not going to quit, and all hell broke out. They continued to threaten to have her institutionalized on the grounds of mental insanity, and threatened her in other ways. I can't speak to what those other threats were, but I can only imagine. She then came by the house to make another appeal in person to have her job back, saying she didn't care what her family thought, she loved her job and loved my daughter. I told her I believed her and that I thought she had done a fine job for us, but it was over. She could never come back.

I was not going to put my child or my family at risk of attack by her racist family. Not only was I concerned about what they might do to us, but I also didn't want my husband's life ruined by what he would do if any of them harmed our baby.

Eventually, we found a new nanny, who was Black. She was great and stayed with us for about a year. After a while, we decided Jeanne-Marie was old enough to go back to day care. So we enrolled her in a facility near our home, one that was highly rated. But then, one evening I came to pick her up and she was not there. Jeanne-Marie was gone.

Trying not to panic, I immediately rushed up to one of the workers and asked where my baby was. That is when I was told they saw bruises on my daughter's back and buttocks and had called Child Protective Services. They said I would have to go over to the hospital where my daughter was being examined and meet with protective services in order to go through the appropriate process to try and get my daughter back. You cannot imagine the level of shock this put me in!

I went to the hospital, frantically trying to find my

daughter. I was directed to the protective services personnel, who were trying to tell me to calm down. But that was not going to happen until I had Jeanne-Marie back in my arms.

They took me to this examination room where the doctor was with my daughter. He walked over to me and placed Jeanne in my arms. He then turned to the protective services people and said this child is healthy and fine. He said the so-called bruises are Mongolian spots, which are congenital birthmarks. This is a very common condition in any part of the body of children of color and can be small or large. They are harmless and usually fade away by school age. I was given a half-assed apology by protective services, and I left holding my daughter tight. But this wasn't over yet.

The next day my husband and I went to meet with the director and staff at the day care center. We let them know in no uncertain terms how upset we were about how we and our child had been treated. We asked if this were a white child, would they have jumped to the immediate conclusion of child abuse, over a flat, non-swollen dark spot on the child? We knew the answer, but we asked anyway. Would you have had protective services come and take the child away from the white parents without even inform-ing or discussing your concerns with them? If you are in the childcare business, why is there no one on your staff who could have been capable of recognizing a common birthmark? We were again given excuses and half-assed apologies. All I could think was that it shouldn't be this hard to work and have a decent amount of peace about who is watching your child. It goes without saying, Jeanne-Marie never went back.

Growing up, I knew Blacks were often punished just for driving, walking, or jogging while Black. But now I had to add "parenting while Black" to the list. These were not problems that my professional white counterparts had to deal with. While this may seem to some to be just a personal anecdote of a negative experience, it represents so much I would experience in corporate America. The Black American often suffers from perpetual assumption. Others assume they know where you are from, what you know, and what you can do. Many assumed I was the lowest on the totem pole, when often my education and experience should have placed me at the top. This was, and remains, a symptom of a larger societal disease. Welcome to Lake Charles!

———————

Okay, so where were we? I was this new Conoco engineer with an office downtown beautifully located in one of the few high-rise buildings in the area. The building was directly across from a peaceful lake and the civic center. During lunch, I would get outside and take in the scenery, feed the ducks, breathe in fresh air, and get a walk in. The office was filled with men dressed in cowboy boots and hats, chewing and spitting tobacco.

In fact, it was common to walk into a coworker's office and find him leaning back in his chair, legs crossed, boots on the tabletop with their tips pointing toward the ceiling.

You would be in mid-conversation and without warning, a colleague would grab a cup and spit in it, leaving remnants struggling to hang on to the bottom lip. It was shocking. It was nasty. I hated it. It was clear, this was a different world.

Not only did I find this practice to be rude, but it was also downright aggressive. It was as though every time I saw someone spit, they seemed to be saying "screw you," but just in a little more descriptive way. I kept my feelings to myself and continued to adjust to this new environment.

I had one boss in particular who went out of his way to make sure I was uncomfortable. Whether we were in my office or his, he would violently cross and uncross his legs. It's hard to explain, but that's about the best way I can explain someone creating unnecessary movement for the purpose of making you feel uncomfortable. He would plop his feet on my desk, lean way back in his chair with his hands behind his head, take his cowboy hat on and off, on and off. He would scratch his head, shaking loose whatever could fall to the floor. He would sit in my chair with an attitude that said, "I dare you to ask me to move." He was being as gross and loud as possible. To make things worse, every discussion with him would be drawn out as long as possible just to let me know that he owned my time. Again, I was adjusting to this new environment, but as with any storm, there is always a ray of light somewhere, and that light was Francisco.

Francisco was another one of my bosses. I remember him because he was nice and respectful—what a novel idea. He made me feel a part of his team. He would walk to

Hardee's with all of us colleagues to have lunch. He didn't chew tobacco, didn't spit in a cup, scratch at random, or put his feet up on the desk while meeting with me. And he helped me out in a sexual harassment situation that could have gone bad really quickly.

To fully operate in my position, I was required to undergo an extensive physical exam and physical skills testing. Thank God I was young, healthy, and had been a cheerleader for many years. One test stands out in my memory. I was required to demonstrate my ability to swing on a rope from the boat-level deck of an offshore platform onto the deck of a work boat. This was important because I was going to be working in the middle of the ocean. Yes, my corporate office was in downtown Lake Charles, but my workplace was really the ocean. The ocean is extremely dangerous. Many lives have been lost on and off the deck of an offshore oil platform. Additionally, drilling and production platforms had been built without considering that a woman would ever be in such a place. I will get back to that in just a bit.

During my physical test, I had the strength and agility to make the swing and land properly. But I must admit, after that training experience, I did everything possible to avoid having to take a boat to or from a platform. I took a helicopter instead. I did this because I suffered terribly from motion sickness. When a boat is tied to the base of a platform with the waves constantly sloshing up and down, the boat follows this motion. The worse the weather, the worse the waves; the worse the motion of the boat, the worse my sickness. There were other tests. I was required to take water survival training. This was to prepare me for dealing with possible emergencies while out in the Gulf of Mexico. The training was held at a huge indoor pool facility in Lafayette, Louisiana. Needless to say, I was the only woman there. This was an experience I will never forget. And the men who heard me screaming during the training will probably never forget either. 😊

One survival exercise was designed to teach me how to survive a helicopter crash into the ocean. I was strapped in a chair with a simulated helicopter door attached to it. First, let me say being strapped to a chair while being lowered into water is mental torture to begin with. They dropped me upside down in the deep end of the pool and left me to my own means to escape. Wow! Can you imagine doing that for your regular corporate America job?! When most people were learning how to use the printer, I was upside down in a pool trying to figure out how in hell I got myself into this position. This exercise was designed to teach me how to unfasten my seat belt, climb through the window of the helicopter, and swim to safety.

Since we're talking about helicopter crashes, this would be a good time to tell you about one that almost happened . . . on purpose. Once I arrived at Conoco, attempts at intimidating me happened on a pretty regular basis. The objective was to make me so afraid that I would "stay in my place," or so fearful that I would conclude this line of work wasn't for me and quit. From the day I arrived in Lake Charles, my time on a helicopter would increase almost weekly. I was in a helicopter as much as other people are in their cars.

Helicopter rides were generally uneventful, that is, if you don't count the sharks swimming beneath you as you fly over. I can remember thinking, "Why get all that helicopter crash survival training if the sharks eat you when you crash?" That aside, one day the pilot assigned to fly me from the platform back to shore had a weird idea of what he thought would be funny. As I climbed the stairs to the helicopter deck, I noticed something. I was the only passenger that day. No problem. I got in.

Everything was fairly normal. The pilot tossed around a bit of small talk. But then, before we took off, he asked me a question. "How afraid are you to fly?" I explained it wasn't too bad and actually rather scenic; and jokingly said with a chuckle that I just tried not to think too much about crashing or sharks. He chatted a little bit more as the blades got faster and faster. I could feel the helicopter beginning to rise from the platform. But then, right as we were about to take off, he turned to me and said, "Well, let's see if you'll still want to fly after this."

Instead of lifting the helicopter up and out over the water, he pointed the nose down straight toward the water and took off. I would have screamed but I couldn't find my voice. I was scared beyond words. All those thoughts about sharks raced through my mind as I watched us headed directly for the ocean. Then suddenly, as if this were a video game, he pulled up at the very last possible second, and we narrowly escaped crashing into the water.

He broke out laughing. "Bet I made you piss your pants," he said.

"Are you crazy?" I asked. "You could have gotten us killed." Then he said arrogantly, "I bet I won't see you in my chopper again."

I quietly thought to myself, *You got that right, but not for the reason you think.*

Once back in the safety of my office, I contacted his helicopter company and had him fired for his reckless and irresponsible behavior. So, he got his wish—he never saw me (or anyone else from Conoco) in his chopper again. I guess that crash survival training isn't a bad idea after all. Another lesson I learned was if an accident ever occurred and I found myself in the water, I would not know which way was up or down. So I was taught to blow bubbles and swim in the direction the bubbles go, because they only flow toward the surface. Simple but important lessons.

One training exercise was designed to teach me how to jump from the top deck of a platform, in case of fire or explosion, all while minimizing injury or worse. The goal was to wrap your arms tight around your chest and keep your body perfectly straight and jump straight down. So, for this exercise, I had to climb to the top of the Olympic-height high-diving board and execute the maneuver. As you can imagine, when it was my turn, all eyes were on me, the Black woman who was about to jump to what seemed like her certain death. As I walked to the edge of the diving board, I just kept thinking, *Gladys, don't panic, you've got this, jump for the culture!* I hesitated, then thought, *Oh hell, it's now or never*, and jumped. I started out in great form. But about halfway down, something happened . . . I lost it! I let out this huge scream and hit the water with a cartoon-like splat. Had the wind knocked out of me. Hurt like hell, but again, I survived.

There are a few more honorable mentions. I was trained in how to rescue an unconscious person by myself by pulling them into a life raft. For this, I was paired with an engineer and friend named Dave, who happened to live across the street from me. Dave was a tall, young, athletic guy, about six foot four. Now imagine his dead weight. All of my Jacksonville, Florida, strength would not have been enough to get Dave into that raft, so he helped me. He threw his body in the raft on my behalf (even though he was supposed to be pretending to be unconscious). Once he was in the raft, I whispered, "You know if this was real, you probably would have drowned." Then he whispered back, "So would a whole lot of other guys—look around the pool." We both broke out laughing.

I was also taught how to trap air in my clothes to stay afloat without a life jacket. I was even taught how to throw your poop away far enough from you in the water so sharks wouldn't be attracted to you. And to think, I never knew sharks liked poop! Welcome to the oil business.

As a production engineer, I did the design and supervised the installation for two new offshore production platforms. I did the design and layout work for the facilities in my office environment. Then I had to spend extended lengths of time down in a huge construction yard on the

West Bank of New Orleans, where the actual platform structure was sitting on land. It was there I supervised the physical construction and installation of processing equipment, controls, operating valves, piping, and so on. Then, once we'd done as much prefabrication as possible, the platform had to be lifted and carried out by barge to its proper location in the middle of the Gulf of Mexico. There the final construction work had to be done on-site, including properly connecting to the well heads and pipelines. Of course, all personnel had to wear hard hats and steel-toed shoes while offshore.

I can remember the great difficulty I had with the first hired crew on my first new platform offshore installation. I had done all this training, but there was no training to navigate hate. When the first crew saw me, they were so annoyed to find out I was their project manager. They went on a mission to be as disrespectful as possible, saying things to me that they never would have said to a male engineer in charge. I had built up some pretty tough skin by then and selectively picked my battles. So, I was just ignoring most of it and continuing to explain what needed to be done and letting them know that we would need to work together as a team to get things done on schedule and budget. The whole time, guys were chewing tobacco and spitting it in cans or spitting overboard, as usual. But this one guy, who had been the most difficult from the moment he laid eyes on me, approached me. Got up in my face. He hacked up this big wad of tobacco spittle and made a show of spitting it on my shoes. The others laughed. I looked at him and said, "I hope that was worth it to you, because you and your entire crew are fired."

I told him he could go wait down on the boat deck for the ride back into shore. I then radioed in and made the necessary arrangements and got a new crew flown out to get to work immediately.

Of course, the new crew had already gotten the word by then that I wouldn't put up with their BS. So, despite a bit of a chip on their shoulders, they didn't want to get fired and generally got on with their jobs. But again, there was still one who just had to find a way to be difficult, but this time in a passive-aggressive way. This guy was a pipe welder. Whenever he saw me coming his direction or knew he was within my eyesight, he would reach and take a sardine out of a can he had sitting nearby and make a show of eating it while he was welding. One should not be eating and welding. I chose to ignore him to see if he would grow tired of the shenanigans once he saw he wasn't getting a rise out of me. He stopped his passive aggression. It seemed I was the engineer, the mother, and supervisor of a group of grown children.

Back to my earlier comment, there were no accommodations made for women in this offshore work environment. On the designated sleeping platforms, the housing units were set up to accommodate four persons to a unit. However, there were no units designated for women. So, whenever I had to stay, that meant they couldn't utilize the three other bunks in the unit. This often caused resentment and animosity. On the production platforms, there were no toilets.

The men would do number one off the side or through the deck grating, straight into the ocean. The men who worked these platforms on a regular basis had generally trained their bodies to not have to do number two until they were back to the sleeping quarters platform. But when nature called, they would do number two in a bucket in what was called the doghouse. The doghouse was a very small, enclosed room housing certain control equipment and was the only place to seek privacy. They would then dump the bucket into the ocean. A key thing about the doghouse is that it had no lock, for safety reasons. You wouldn't want to have a worker on the platform alone and accidentally get locked inside the unit.

To be honest, if I absolutely had to go number two, I would call for a helicopter and fly back to the quarter's platform to use the toilet. But if it was just number one, then I used the bucket in the doghouse. But that's not the worst of it. Sometimes, while sitting on the bucket, the men—who knew I was sitting on the bucket—would "mistakenly" push open the door just to embarrass me. They would then offer a fake apology as I tried to finish my business. Welcome to Lake Charles!

Back on shore, there were many times when I, along with a group of Conoco employees, would travel for business. When we traveled for business, as soon as the official business or workday was over, the guys seemed to have one mission: get as drunk as they could as fast as they could and misbehave. I'm sure that has a lot to do with why to this day I have a very low tolerance for being around drunk people.

One incident I have never forgotten is when I traveled to an oil show in Lafayette with some of the engineers from my office. We drove together in one of the company cars. Lafayette was only about an hour and a half away from our Lake Charles office. So we were supposed to drive back home after the show, instead of spending the night. However, this didn't stop the engineers from getting totally drunk and behaving ridiculously. Naturally, I had to do the driving because the guys were drunk.

But just trying to get all of them to leave and get in the car was bad enough. Once you find one, another one disappears. It was like herding cats.

I start driving down the highway, when one of the guys begins to yell, "Stop the car! Stop the car! I have to pee right now!" I'm like, *you have got to be kidding me.* Then others chime in, "You have to stop now!"

As fast as I could, I pulled off the highway and onto the shoulder of the road. But before I can fully stop, one guy jumps out on the passenger side and just starts peeing out toward the highway. Then, after the car has come to a complete stop, a guy on the driver side attempts to get out to pee. He trips and stumbles as he gets out, and somehow several beer cans roll out of the car or his lap and fall into the highway and start rolling across toward the center lane, and we have to grab him and keep him from getting himself run over.

Then, when the free-for-all pee marathon and comedy show was over, it was back to herding laughing cats back into the car. Can you even conceive of this happening in a business situation today, much less in the presence of a female? This, my friend, was my introduction into the bowels of the oil industry during the late 1970s, early '80s in Lake Charles, Louisiana. But wait—there's more.

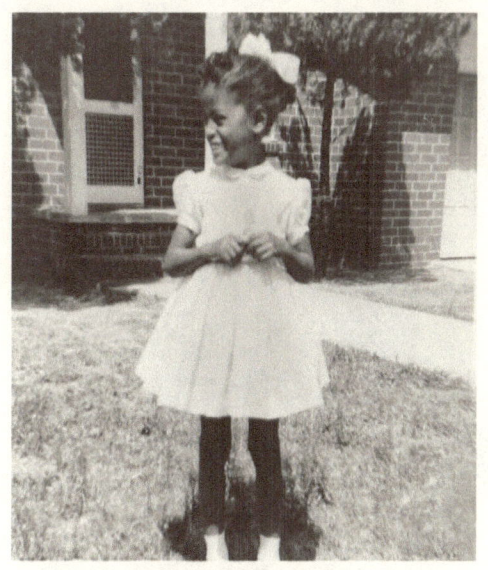

Gladys on an Easter Sunday

Gladys—High school cheerleader

1985—Gladys and daughter, during MBA school in Madison, WI

Gladys and other attendees, at a British
Petroleum Management Conference at Leeds Castle in England

2006—Headshot for YWCA Award Program

BLACK ENTERPRISE

Caribbean Business Opportunities

YOUR ULTIMATE SOURCE FOR WEALTH CREATION   FEBRUARY 2009

100

Most Powerful Executives

In Corporate America

10 Affordable Home-based Franchises
You Should Buy Now!

Women & Money
Financial Advice For
Every Stage Of Life

OUR BEST AND BRIGHTEST
Gladys DeClouet, Derica Rice,
Adriane M. Brown, and Reed V. Tuckson

2009—Magazine cover

2017—60th birthday with granddaughters

8

The Party, the German, and the Boot

As a reservoir engineer at Conoco, my role expanded beyond the production platforms to the buzzing world of drilling rigs. These rigs, larger and teeming with workers, represented my new territory. And it was here my challenges intensified. The absence of designated facilities for women was just the tip of the iceberg. Longer work schedules for the field workers, sometimes stretching thirty days at sea, bred an environment where sexual harassment wasn't just present, it was rampant, and I would go as far as to say almost encouraged by the culture. On overnight stays, which I kept to a minimum, I slept fully clothed in a chair in the rig foreman's office.

This period of my career was a test of endurance, both physically and emotionally. I had to constantly assert my worth and my right to be there, amid an environment that seemed hell-bent on proving otherwise. My work involved designing oil well drilling plans, evaluating the results of oil and gas discoveries, assessing economic feasibilities, completing reserve studies, and negotiating complex sharing agreements with competing companies. I was routinely making multimillion-dollar decisions. All of this required a keen mind and a resilient spirit, qualities I had in abundance but often went unrecognized due to the cultural and gender biases around me.

My personal life, in contrast, was a respite of love and support. Michael and I met under the most serendipitous circumstances, a chance encounter that led to marriage and a family together. It was the summer before my senior year of college. I had just purchased a Toyota and then immediately hit the road, driving from Jacksonville, Florida, to Lake Charles, Louisiana, for a summer engineering job with Conoco. As I approached Lake Charles, a service light came on in my car. I got nervous and wanted to find a Toyota dealership. I started driving cautiously and looking around to see where to seek help. Out of nowhere, a handsome man appeared like a phoenix out of the service light ashes. He was standing in front of the Buick/Oldsmobile dealership. I had to think fast.

For one, this wasn't a Toyota dealership, but I figured hey, a car is a car, right? I made a split-second decision and turned in, pulling right up to the space next to my phoenix man.

"Hi, can you tell me where my future, I mean my Toyota dealership, is?"

The rest is history. We were together every day for the rest of that summer. Michael's presence in my life was a constant reminder of the goodness and beauty amid the ugliness of my professional world.

Once our daughter, Jeanne-Marie, arrived, I imparted the lessons of equality, self-belief, and resilience. I imagined one day she may be in the position I was in, yet hoping the world would be different by the time my little girl was an adult. I felt it my responsibility to prepare her as if nothing was ever going to change. Jeanne-Marie needed to have all I had and more. I wrote a message in her baby book encapsulating the wisdom I had gathered: the importance of self-worth, the courage to pursue one's goals, and the ability to love fully and trust wisely. This is the letter I penned:

Always remember that no other human being is better than you are. We are all equal children of God. Believe in yourself and have the confidence to go after and accomplish whatever worthwhile goals you may have in your life. Never subdue to intimidation.

Jeanne-Marie, I hope you are blessed with the instinct to know who to trust and be faithful to. But I also hope you can learn to love fully.

Jeanne-Marie, I love you.
Mom

An engineering role with Conoco requires quite a bit of ongoing training, which the company was great at providing. Specifically, the training I received at their ranch in Ponca City, Oklahoma, was a mix of technical learning and harrowing experiences. As the only female attendee, I was often the target of pranks and inappropriate behavior. One incident in particular stood out—an attempted assault by a field foreman named Smitty.

Remember that knock on the bedroom door I referenced earlier? Let me finish that story for you. It was during one particular training course at the ranch, where we had engineers and field management personnel in attendance. Things got a little out of hand. The guys had been teasing me and pulling small pranks, which I just ignored. That night after dinner, they seemed exceptionally rowdy. One guy in particular, a field foreman, was drinking excessively. I decided to turn in early. Now, my room was on the second floor of the bunkhouse about halfway down the walkway.

My German friend Joe walked me back to my room. He told me to be careful because he had heard Smitty—the field foreman—downstairs bragging about what he was going to do to me. I thanked him for the heads-up, went into my room, and closed the door behind me.

It wasn't long until I heard a knock at my door. I assumed it was Joe turning back to tell me something, so I just opened the door. It was Smitty, standing there like something out of a horror movie. He immediately put his cowboy boot in the doorway, leaning forward with his arm against the door to stop me from closing it. I told him to leave. He said not before he got what he wanted. Instead of trying to close the door, I opened it fully and as he fell forward into the room, I quickly ran down the walkway. I started to loudly tell him to get out of my room. Joe heard the commotion and came back running toward me. He forced Smitty to leave. I returned to my room, locked the door, and remained in for the night.

This experience, along with another disturbing incident involving a dead reptile, compelled me to report these occurrences to headquarters. It was a moment of reckoning, one that reinforced my resolve to stand against such behavior.

The way the division manager handled the situation with Smitty was a lesson in what leadership should not be. He had me, a young engineer, decide the fate of the long-tenured foreman, who was my assaulter, while I sat in front of both of them. I was fairly new and only twenty-three years old, facing the head of the Lake Charles Exploration and Production Division. So, it is not surprising that I said

I would be okay if he didn't fire my assaulter, who was sitting there whining about how he needed to keep his job in order to take care of his wife and kids.

This was a glaring example of abdication and poor leadership—the kind I would never emulate. This shaped my own leadership style. I vowed to be the kind of leader who stands up for her employees, ensures a safe working environment, and makes the tough calls.

During my years with Conoco, I gained excellent experience and learned many valuable lessons and skills. I contributed within the company and to the industry. My professional activities in Lake Charles included serving at various times as board member, second vice chairman, and membership chair of the Society of Petroleum Engineers of AIME, as well as vice president of the Louisiana Engineering Alliance Program for Minorities.

My journey through these tumultuous years was a testament to resilience and the relentless pursuit of justice and equality. Each challenge, each setback, and each victory shaped me into a leader who not only excelled in her field but also stood for integrity and strength. Mine was not just a career; it was a journey of transformation, a path that changed my future paths. No matter the position, the money, or the accolades, I would be guided by a moral compass that never wavered.

I finally decided to leave Conoco at a pivotal moment. The relocation of our division office to Lafayette coincided with my growing interest in the financial and economic aspects of the industry. I saw an opportunity to shift my career trajectory and seized it. I enrolled in the MBA program at the University of Wisconsin, a decision fueled by my passion and facilitated by a full fellowship based on my academic and professional merits.

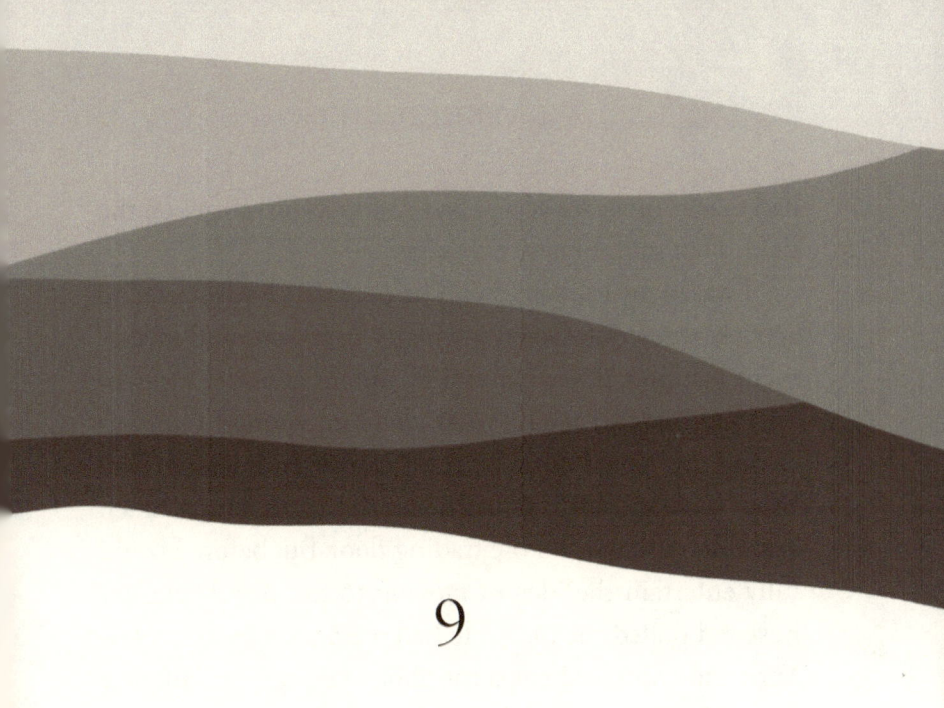

9

Oil in the Water

Just walk around the campus of any MBA school toward the end of the last semester . . . now look up in the sky. Do you see them? Vultures are circling. There is corporate blood in the water, or in my case, there was oil in the water. Companies show up at just the right time to scoop up fresh meat: talented students who may or may not know their value in the marketplace. MBA graduates are like college athletes. We want to be drafted by a professional team so bad that at times we accept bad contracts just to get on the field. That said, I knew my value.

I was in my last semester. The corporate birds started to actively reach out. Given my major in finance and investment banking, it was natural for me to consider a career on Wall Street. I mean, what could go wrong? This was during the "greed is good" era. I can't even imagine Wall Street having a women's bathroom during that time, much less a Black female on the trading floor. But before I could fully entertain the idea of moving to the Big Apple, my husband pulled the plug. He had previously lived in New York and expressed concerns about raising our daughter there. Thus, I took another path.

My top two job offers were from Procter & Gamble (in Cincinnati) and The Standard Oil Company (in Cleveland). P&G had a longstanding relationship with Tuskegee University, and other Tuskegee alums who worked there were enthusiastic about their workplace. But Standard Oil made it difficult for me to turn down their offer. My prior knowledge in the oil industry, coupled with my engineering degree, as well as having recently earned my master's in business from the University of Wisconsin, made me an invaluable asset to any oil company.

Standard Oil initially spotted my résumé when I began my MBA program, in the book of scholarship recipients for both the Consortium for Graduate Studies in Management and the National Black MBA Association. They kept tabs on me and my progress. I was inducted into the Beta Gamma Sigma Honor Society, selected into Outstanding Young

Women of America 1985, and graduated with a grade point average of 3.8 on a 4-point scale, despite my concurrent mother and wife responsibilities. Standard Oil was impressed.

At the start of my final semester, they reached out with an encouraging message. Looking back, it was like online dating before online dating was created. I was being courted. They invited me to an interview, where among other people, I met Jim Schaefer, the hiring manager. I felt that Jim genuinely respected me, saw my potential, and wanted to see me succeed.

They made me an incredible offer and invited my family and me to visit Cleveland. They treated us like they wanted to get married and live happily ever after!

They provided wonderful accommodations. Specifically, a luxurious suite at Stouffer's Hotel in Tower City Downtown—with limousine access to boot. We enjoyed dinner at the HR manager's home. (My first time trying crème brûlée—let's just say crème brûlée wasn't a Southern dish. ☺) On top of all that, Standard Oil paid for my husband to work with a placement service to find him a job. In the end, I said yes to their proposal. Also, Jim soon became a mentor to me, someone I respected and admired.

When I joined Standard Oil, they were still benefiting from impacts of the oil boom and were experiencing huge profits. They had recently built an opulent headquarters building—the "marble tower" as Clevelanders affectionately refer to it—downtown on Public Square opposite Cleveland's famed Tower City. It was a little bit of New York in the Midwest.

Even though crude oil prices had fallen sharply in 1986, the environment remained highly profitable and exciting throughout my tenure in the oil industry. One advantage of working with an oil company with a fully integrated business model is this: Even when profits in one segment of your business are being squeezed, you are still making profits (often increased profits) across other areas. To be fully integrated, in layman's terms, just means that the same company that produces the raw product also refines the product, distributes and markets the product, and then sells the product to the end consumer. They own every profit center along the chain.

As an engineer at Conoco (and later Conoco/DuPont after the merger), I worked in what was known as the upstream side of the oil industry, which focused primarily on exploration and production activities, including onshore and offshore drilling of oil and gas wells. Later, after earning my MBA and joining Standard Oil/BP Oil, I worked in what was known as the downstream side of the business, which ultimately brings usable products to end users and consumers. It includes operations such as crude oil trading, pipeline transportation, refining, storage, marketing, truck distribution, retail stations, and so on.

Though not as outwardly chauvinistic or racist as its *upstream* counterpart, some aspects of the *downstream* oil industry still had pervasive issues. It was still a man's world. How did it get this way? Well, there are many contributing factors, but not unlike many industries in the US, those who first experience success become the image of what success in that industry looks like. For right or for wrong, the first winner often becomes the standard in race and gender for all who come behind.

For context, let me share a quick synopsis of the history of the big and powerful US oil companies. In 1911, the Supreme Court ruled that John D. Rockefeller's Standard Oil Company had become so big and so powerful that it was determined to be an illegal monopoly. The court divided Standard Oil into forty-three distinct entities based on region and activity, some of which kept using Standard Oil's name (e.g., Standard Oil of New Jersey, California, New York, or Ohio). Then, after World War II, many mergers, acquisitions, and name changes took place to form companies such as Exxon, Mobil, Chevron, Conoco, Amoco, and so on, until by 1986 Standard Oil of Ohio (Sohio) was the sole entity left with Standard Oil in their name. They then rebranded in 1986 from Sohio to The Standard Oil Company the year I joined them and began my career at the marble tower office in Cleveland.

But things started to change fast. After I joined The Standard Oil Company in 1986, British Petroleum purchased it in 1987 and it became BP Oil, part of the second-largest oil company in the world. Cleveland headquarters became their American headquarters. It was then that I began to face racism and sexism not only from American culture, but also from the British, which added classism to the list. It was a toxic cocktail of skin and bloodline bias, the likes of which I had never experienced. Black Americans understand good ole Southern racism. It is clear and without confusion. But the British form is more intellectual than emotional and, dare I say, it is even more potentially damaging to some. But I did not let it deter me. Life comes in layers: It was the best of times and it was the worst of times.

Not long after my graduation, job offer, and successful new career start, my world fell apart. My twenty-eight-year-old brother, Lenard—one year younger than me and the closest of all my siblings—tragically passed away in a car accident. It is difficult for me to even write this. I will never forget that phone ringing late at night and my sister Paula screaming and weeping on the other end.

My world came to a sudden stop. Lenard had only recently asked if he could come visit for a while, but my mom had advised against it at that time. Though I knew intellectually that I couldn't have changed his fate, my guilt for not letting him come visit right away tortured me for years. Even to this day, my worst nightmare is hearing the phone ring in the middle of the night—it incites anxiety and indescribable fear.

Just months after my brother passed, my stepfather, whom I loved and who was the only father I had ever known, passed away at age fifty-three from heart failure, as a result of high blood pressure.

It was all so tragic. Yet despite my grief, my focus turned toward my mom. She had just lost her son and husband within months of each other. It felt almost like déjà vu of when she lost both of her sisters within months of each other during my senior year of college. It was all too much.

Even today, I can only discuss it for a certain amount of time before depression knocks on my door.

During my twelve years at BP, my focus was on climbing the corporate ladder. To their credit, I received plenty of developmental support and opportunities. I gained experiences across different functions and roles within all segments of downstream operations, which gave me an in-depth knowledge base as well as various skills, competencies, and leadership capabilities.

Despite not having an Ivy League background, I ended up having an Ivy League experience. Early in my tenure with BP, I was identified as a high-potential employee and was included in the Internal Development Program (IDP), an exclusive initiative for select groups of employees. Many employees, particularly Black employees, are unaware that such programs exist within corporations. But they exist throughout corporate America in all shapes and sizes; they often go by other names, such as Fast Track. These programs typically support various succession-planning initiatives to guarantee a pipeline of future leaders within the company.

Candidates for these programs gain a certain breadth and depth of experiences and skills. Typically, candidates deemed to have high potential are placed in the program and are removed if their performance falls short of expectations. From BP's IDP, I received progressive levels of the Group Leadership course (stages 1 and 2), Targeted Management, Positive Power and Influence, as well as presentation skills. These courses helped me refine my natural talents.

My initial three years with BP were spent in the Crude Oil Trading and Transportation Group. My first job was as a planning analyst, making me responsible for determining when and what crude to purchase, trade, or sell in order to maximize profits. It was a little bit of Wall Street, you could say. We attended morning briefing meetings where we reviewed market updates and made plans for the trading day ahead. The office atmosphere was much friendlier than in my upstream days with Conoco.

However, there was still an overindulging and drinking culture. When attending business lunches and after-work events with coworkers and crude oil traders, the level of alcohol consumption was unbelievable. Even my British supervisor encouraged me to fake drink in order to fit in. I learned how to fill a glass with alcohol, or something that looked like alcohol, and nurse that thing for an hour or two. There is a science to doing it in a way that no one noticed. But I will spare you the boring details.

One year later, I was promoted to business development manager within our Lower 48 States Pipeline Group. Here, I collaborated with partner oil companies and customers of jointly owned petroleum product pipelines in order to boost transportation sales and maximize system utilization. This part of the business was a throwback to an older era, especially when dealing with the crude oil pipeline companies out of Longview, Texas. There was plenty of condescension and attempts at being dismissive or demeaning by the business associates I had to work with.

As part of my role within the pipelines group, I was

given a stretch assignment, which added the position of manager of financial analysis for our Alaskan crude oil business. This meant I held both responsibilities as controller for Alaskan pipeline operations and business development manager for Lower 48 States Pipeline Group activities. Me, a Black woman.

Holding two jobs simultaneously presented some unique challenges; it was both mentally challenging and physically demanding. My two offices were several floors apart on opposite sides of the building and in different elevator banks from each other. Hustling back and forth during the day proved to be quite taxing. It was like a daily marathon.

Oh—and yeah, I became pregnant during this time. So, imagine a pregnant woman waddling up and down hallways all day from one side of the building to the other. Then, due to my preeclampsia, I was placed on bed rest for several weeks until it was determined that the baby would be healthy enough to be delivered without undue risk. Thankfully, my mother-in-law came to the rescue and stayed with me until I could resume full activity. It was quite an ordeal.

Our son chose to be born on my husband's birthday, which was a gift from on high! Michael joked that he would age no more because he was now giving his birthdays to his son, Bradford (Brad). I joked that I no longer had to get him birthday gifts because I had just given him a gift for life. We both won! But in all honesty, I actually saw the biggest benefit to having my son's birth delayed until my husband's birthday was that it gave me time to attend Michael Jackson's "Bad" concert! I know, random, right?

My husband and I went with our hospital bag packed just in case, but I couldn't pass up this chance to witness one of music's all-time great performers! Michael didn't disappoint. We danced the night away while I was in the audience, nine months pregnant, singing along to MJ's "I'm Bad!"

And if I can say so myself, I was pretty bad. 😊

10

The Missing Video

When I sat down to note career highlights for my next nine years with BP, from 1989 to 1998, my notes looked more like a résumé than an experience. Don't get me wrong, what I accomplished is something I consider a blessing. But many times, the conditions under which I made strides were far more telling than the strides I made.

Working for a corporation as large and dynamic as British Petroleum is a mixed bag. By any measurement, the lifestyle

I led during these years was a great one. I experienced so many wonderful things. But as you may imagine, there were bad things as well. I have come to learn: You simply cannot separate the two. Maybe there should be something called a "résumé of challenges": a document that digs deep not just into your accomplishments, but also the obstacles you scaled while still being productive. It could just be me, but the test of a true leader is not necessarily that they are smart, empathetic, have appropriate levels of shrewd decision-making skills, are competent, and listen, but that maybe they have to do all of these things while undergoing chemotherapy. Maybe growing a division by ten times its historical annual revenue would mean even more if this leader buried her child in the midst of all of it. There is something to be said for what we go through while accomplishing our goals.

Here are a few notes on my other positions and responsibilities at BP:

- Ultimately achieved a glass-ceiling breakthrough job into the executive suite, as division manager for the Cleveland Division
  - » Responsible for the P&L (profit and loss) of all sales through all channels of trade within BP's Cleveland geographic division, which also included all retail gas stations and convenience stores
  - » Had sales and profit increases each year, along with improvements in other operational and customer performance metrics

- » Top Performance Award—BP World Class Performance Program
- » Won BP's Top Safety Award two years in a row, achieving two million work hours without any lost-time accidents
- Achieved a barrier breakthrough role in operations management, as region manager in terminals and distribution
  - » Oversaw the receipt, storage, handling, and delivery of billions of gallons per year of petroleum products
- Manager of planning for the Americas, in BP's International Aviation Fuels Division
  - » Developed business strategies for airline and general aviation sales, and acquisition & development of fixed-based operations; managed Management Information Systems Development Team
- Founding member of BP's Diversity Council
  - » Developed a diversity training program that all BP America employees attended, and I personally attended with the CEO and the most senior leaders
  - » Influenced the launch of a corporate-wide major culture change effort
- Received *Kaleidoscope* magazine's Young Corporate Leaders Award and was inducted

into the Cleveland 40/40 Club, recognizing outstanding people under the age of forty in achievement and community contributions

- Participated in many internal and external volunteer activities to help mentor and develop others, such as Minorities in Engineering Program; INROADS; Career Beginnings; Consortium for Graduate Studies in Management; Big Brothers Big Sisters; Junior Achievement; Cleveland State University National Technical Association

This list doesn't tell you the story behind the curtain. It doesn't let you in on the personalities I had to navigate or how many things were said to me without using words. The atmosphere in a room can speak much louder than words. The list also doesn't take you between the lines, where so many great and magical things took place. When you are working so hard to achieve, you often lose sight of the impact you are having not only in real time, but for years to come with people you will never meet. My professional life was really a blueprint for a building that was to be completed at a later date. I was there to lay a firm foundation.

But, if you take away from this that my time was a challenge with few smiles or enjoyment, you have misunderstood me. Let me put it plainly. I had fun! I went places, met people, and did things few people on earth can say they have done. One such experience was when

I spent three weeks touring Australia and New Zealand with a private plane assigned to transport me around to various airport facilities.

This was when I was the manager of planning for the Americas region in BP's International Aviation Fuels Division and had been tasked with leading the development of BP's worldwide general aviation strategy.

While enjoying flying private down under, I stayed in a big hotel casino in Perth, Australia, and was invited to come up and spend time in the high-rollers gambling room. Told you I had fun! The room was full of wealthy Japanese placing million-dollar bets. I remember the room being eerily quiet. I just sipped champagne and observed. There's more from this same trip. I found myself in the middle of a gold mine in the Outback of Australia. Not bad for a young girl from Jacksonville, Florida.

There was also the proposal presentation to the BP Oil worldwide CEO. That presentation was in London. It was to sell the idea of buying the company's first fixed-base operation (FBO) at a general aviation airport—the Atlanta DeKalb-Peachtree Airport. This meeting was actually the kickoff for BP's FBO acquisition strategy, but here's the fun part: I was flown to London in a first-class sleeper cabin. Picked up by a Mercedes limo and driven to my private bathroom and dressing room. Women like private bathrooms, in case you didn't know.

I was rushed straight out of there into the boardroom to make my presentation. My travel partner, who was also a part of the project but not the presenter, had a death in his family and had to be flown out immediately on the Concorde—yes, that Concorde. I was so mentally and physically exhausted from the stress and excitement that I spent that night just sleeping, instead of celebrating the success of the project and enjoying London. And all of this was done as a thirty-three-year-old Black female from Jacksonville, Florida, back in 1990.

These experiences were invaluable. I traveled all over the world and got to know different cultures, which sharpened my understanding of the business world in general. Another of my listed positions was region manager in terminals and distribution (T&D), overseeing petroleum product operations in Ohio and Michigan. Let me take you behind the veil of this opportunity for just a peek.

This job made me responsible for the receipt, storage, and handling of billions of gallons of petroleum products at eight terminal and distribution facilities in Ohio and Michigan, including the truck delivery of nearly two billion gallons per year. Yes, two billion. My direct reports were the terminal managers. But the organization I was responsible for included union, company, and contract personnel. The objective was to run smooth and efficient operations to maximize profits. But an even bigger goal was to get the job done safely.

So, imagine now having trucks carrying nine thousand gallons of gasoline out on the road in the middle of a blizzard, or hearing there has been a truck rollover and they don't yet have the status of the driver, or a possible fire in or near a petroleum product storage tank. The stress could

be unbelievable. And as the leader, ensuring safe operations was my responsibility. There's an odd dynamic in the
distribution of credit in executive ranks. If something goes
well, it was a team effort; but if something goes wrong, it's
your fault. I am glad to say that my organization had an
excellent safety record for accidents and lost-time injuries.

Remember the atmosphere that speaks so loudly,
which I mentioned earlier? This job, region manager in
terminals and distribution, was one of those positions. I
was not welcomed when I first received the promotion.
As with the entire oil industry, this division was good ole
boy in its operation style. For example, on my first day
on the job, my boss made it clear to me that if he had his
choice, I wouldn't be there. But thank goodness, my boss's
boss and other people in the decision-making process had
better judgment and faith in me. The backstory I later
heard was that the person I replaced was a man who had
been from one of our international offices, and it seems
the boss was happy to be done with that foreigner and was
ready to "get things back to normal." In general, however,
a Black female in this level of a leadership position in
the oil industry didn't represent "normal" by any stretch
of the imagination.

Over time, my boss and I got to know each other better, went to a few lunches, and created a professional bond.
What the Black female executive, who has been given a
unique opportunity, soon finds out is this: You must prove
your humanity, your competence, and even your ability
to be comfortable as a scapegoat. We do not walk in the

door enjoying the assumptions others enjoy, and it is that absence of positive assumption that will eventually make you great, or make you leave.

But it was my next position that truly had me break the glass ceiling. Not only did it leapfrog me beyond an entry-level C-suite position, but it put me in the role of running a large corporate business unit with accountability for its P&L. My last role was already quite an achievement with running a major operating expense unit. But now I was responsible for achieving both the sales and revenue goals, and the operational expense goals—that is, the total profit and loss. This was truly rock-star status for a woman in corporate America at that time, and especially in the oil industry.

Being accountable for the profit and loss as the new division manager for the Cleveland Division taught me many lessons. Those above you expect a certain kind of tolerance for inconvenience. Those above you expect you to have an ability to withstand offense, to be tough-skinned at all times. Those above you want to know the answer to one question: How much money did we make this quarter? I learned invaluable lessons about what matters to a corporation of BP's size and influence.

Thankfully, BP also celebrated when we did well. We worked hard, but played just as hard. BP Oil had an annual World Class Sales Contest and Awards Program. Based on a specific set of criteria, a certain number of the top-performing dealers and franchisees in the world for that fiscal year would be awarded as BP World Class Winners and would be treated to an extravagant world-class trip. The overall top-performing sales division would also be declared World Class Winners, and that leadership team would get to go on the trip and attend the festivities. This was a coveted award.

In 1995, my Cleveland Division team won the World Class contest and the right for my division leadership team and me to attend and be corporate hosts for the trip.

Well, it turned out that due to various circumstances, the SVP of sales and marketing and the president of BP Oil were not able to make the trip that year. So I ended up being the senior executive and official host for the entire trip and World Class events. Can you feel the room changing? There was also a videographer who had been sent to film throughout the trip and make a highlights video for everyone to take home for a keepsake memory. This was a standard practice for these types of events.

This was a good thing for me. My team was the top performer for the first year of my job, and I was the single team executive host for a very prestigious event. All the planets were lining up. The trip was to Athens, Greece, for a few days, followed by a cruise with stops at the various Greek Islands. I poured myself into it and made sure to make everyone feel honored and welcomed. I kicked off and attended all the activities and presented the awards during the recognition dinner. It was a great time.

But remember, life comes in layers, and the good cannot be separated from the bad. When the trip was over, my team and I returned home happy and feeling great. And then here comes the kick in the gut! When the video keepsake of the trip was sent out to everyone, I was conspicuously missing from it. I, the senior host of the trip, who normally would have been seen in abundance in this type of a video, was not included. Tell me, how was I supposed to believe that could have been unintentional? I remained quiet about it for a while. But then I spoke up to the appropriate people. A member of our senior leadership team apologized to me on behalf of the company for this blatant slight. He was a good and supportive guy, and I am sure his apology and regret were sincere. But the trip could not be redone, and events would never be filmed again with me in the same position. I would never be in the video.

Yes, I accepted the apology, but the truth is, I may never know the truth.

11

Thinking Out of the Box

I am confident my career would have continued to rise at BP. But after twelve years, the time came for me to move on. BP asked me to stay, but I was aggressively recruited. Plus, leaving the dreary weather of Cleveland for the sunshine of Southern California was too hard to resist. My next move would not be to a vertical business, or even within the oil and gas industry. Instead, I headed in an entirely different direction.

I should mention something that is not often said, especially to young professionals. You may find your greatest value when you apply your skills outside of the box you have become accustomed to. Transferring your abilities to an industry unfamiliar with your perspective can be magical.

Many generations now have operated under a résumé mentality—a chronological sequence of professional positions that adds credibility or at least qualifies a person to move into a higher position in that same industry. But as is often the case, the counterintuitive option is the most ignored yet most valuable decision-making strategy in business. In the oil and gas industry I learned so much about oil and gas production, refineries, the customer-facing part of the business, and the behind-the-veil integration that makes BP what it is. But I also learned how to manage at the executive level, how to successfully execute operations worth hundreds of millions of dollars, how to identify talent that just needs grooming, and a host of other aspects that can best be described as nuances. When you learn these skills in a particular industry, their greatest value can, arguably, be found when you go into an unrelated industry.

In the unrelated industry, your ideas will be viewed as fresh and innovative because your angle of understanding originates from a foreign place. You understand business enough to advance the bottom line, but your experience will be unlike that of anyone in this new location. It's the best of both worlds. I say all that to say this: When I left

BP, I took an executive position at—wait for it—Jack in the Box. I migrated from oil and gas to the food service industry. And what a story it was.

This was an interesting leap, transitioning from the intricacies of oil and gas to the bustling world of Jack in the Box (JACK). By way of background, JACK is a renowned American fast-food chain with a widespread footprint. With its 2,200 locations primarily gracing the West Coast and Hawaii, JACK has also managed to establish a considerable presence in various urban centers ranging from Phoenix to Indianapolis.

Before my entrance in 1998, the company had faced its own set of challenges, and that is putting it mildly. In 1993, five years before my arrival, JACK had to grapple with a corporate crisis that nearly sent the company into bankruptcy. Undercooked burger patties led to an E. coli outbreak, tragically taking the lives of four children in the state of Washington. The event severely damaged the brand's image. However, the story of resilience that followed was nothing short of inspiring. Not only did JACK survive, but it also pioneered key shifts in food-safety protocols, benefiting both the US and the world.

By the time I was approached to join the team, the company was entering its "Jack's Back" marketing campaign. The focus? Revitalize the brand. In the nine years that followed my induction, JACK's sales soared to a staggering three-and-a-half billion dollars ($6.6 billion in 2025 dollars). Unlike many other prominent chains, a significant majority of JACK outlets remained company-owned, around

80 to 85 percent. But times were changing, and so was the industry model, as it transitioned toward a predominantly franchised structure. As a point of reference, today more than 90 percent of JACK's outlets are franchised.

The JACK I entered had a deep-rooted culture, one where longevity was celebrated. It was a place where employees traditionally believed you had to be born and raised within the company's walls to truly understand its essence. My hiring, therefore, marked a distinctive shift. I was the third person ever to be recruited above the area manager level from outside, and the very first from a non-restaurant background.

I still fondly remember my interview conversation with my would-be boss. He had been curious about my capability to seamlessly transition from the big-money oil industry to the small-margin, highly competitive quick-serve restaurant industry. I told him that to me, it was all about leadership and delivering products and services through people and systems. The commodities might differ—gasoline and diesel fuel at BP, hamburgers and fries at JACK—but the essence remained the same. I could tell by his reaction to my response that he was impressed and that the deal was sealed. 😊

My tenure at JACK was characterized by brand rejuvenation. I became the first woman to hold a pivotal P&L position within the company, and my initiatives were met with accolades, like the YWCA 27th Annual Award to Women and Industry in 2006. My commitment to nurturing talent bore fruit as well; many past and still current leaders at JACK were once under my mentorship, including a chairman and CEO.

Given my background at BP, JACK also trusted me with the task of pioneering a convenience store concept, aimed at leveraging premium real estate locations too costly for standalone restaurants. With a passionate director at my side, we crafted a contemporary, appealing initiative.

I started my Jack in the Box journey as the regional vice president for the Los Angeles region, the company's most significant and profitable region. I knew that the region's success depended as much on its leader as on the support of the team. To gain the necessary credibility and understanding, I immersed myself in an intense eight-week onboarding process—working restaurant shifts, visiting other regions, and spending time with key people from all the corporate departments. I met with each member of the leadership team in my own region to understand their issues and priorities, and most importantly, I asked everyone what I could do to make them more successful. This hands-on approach allowed me to resonate with the ethos of the company and created respect and team loyalty from the outset.

Contrary to the preconceptions of corporate headquarters, I did not have to conduct a massive bloodshed of regional staff who were believed to be burned out and had bad attitudes. Instead, I was able to revitalize and realign the existing team in ways that best utilized the various strengths of individuals and provided new and exciting roles and experiences for many. This way, we were able to maintain the massive amount of experience and knowledge in our highly tenured employees, and we ended up with a totally reenergized, enthusiastic team that quickly delivered the top operational and profit performance in the company, and at sustained, unprecedented levels for many years.

Leading the "culture under construction" initiative, I championed the service-profit chain, an ideology I still firmly believe in. In essence, when employees are nurtured and cared for, they in turn elevate the customer experience, leading to the brand's profitability. This is important. When you treat your employees the way you want your employees to treat your customers, everyone wins.

After only eighteen months of heading the Los Angeles region, I was promoted to divisional VP. Then a year later, I was promoted to a corporate officer and vice president of operations, where I continued to build high-performance teams at JACK. A few of my accomplishments were:

- Directly responsible for P&L of $2 billion ($3.8 billion in 2025 dollars) per year sales operation from over nine hundred company-owned and -operated restaurants and seventy convenience store and fuel locations, with approximately thirty thousand employees

- Member of leadership council responsible for strategic direction and performance of entire corporation with $3.5 billion ($6.6 billion in 2025 dollars) per year in sales

- Successfully improved sales and profits each year, some in the double digits

- A vital player in leading JACK's successful brand reinvention and culture change efforts
- Stock price more than tripled during position tenure, with direct responsibility for 65 to 80 percent of company's total profit
- Legacy of finding and developing great talent
- Received YWCA 27th Annual Award to Women and Industry
- Led collaborative and smooth acquisition and re-franchising deals
- Participated in professional organizations and activities, including board of directors, Jack in the Box Foundation; board of directors, March of Dimes, San Diego–Imperial Division; WFF (Women in Food Service Forum); MFHA (Multicultural Foodservice and Hospitality Alliance); MUFSO (Multi-Unit Foodservice Operators); NRA (National Restaurant Association); (BBBS) Big Brothers Big Sisters of America; Junior Achievement

It was evident that the cornerstone of our success was the team culture. People often ask, "What's the secret to building such a powerful, cohesive team?" It goes beyond mere strategy and performance metrics. It boils down to a deep-rooted belief in the power of inclusivity, trust, and mutual respect.

Inclusivity: Our leadership teams had a diversity of

backgrounds, gender, ethnicities, and so on. This wasn't just a mere token gesture. We believed that the more diverse our leadership, the broader our perspective and the richer our solutions. By embracing a myriad of backgrounds, experiences, and worldviews, we were better equipped to serve our diverse clientele and understand the needs and aspirations of our diverse staff.

Trust: Our leadership was built on trust. If a member of our team stumbled, we were there to pick them up, not point fingers. This culture of trust encouraged risk-taking and innovation. It made our team feel secure, knowing they were supported even in their mistakes.

Mutual Respect: Respect wasn't a buzzword; it was a lived experience. Whether dealing with a fresh recruit or a veteran manager, respect was non-negotiable. It was the foundation stone upon which all our interactions were built.

As we traveled the journey, there were highs and lows, celebrations and challenges. But the collective vision of Jack in the Box was clear—to be an industry leader, not just in terms of sales and growth, but in terms of its values and culture.

With my relocation to the Jack in the Box headquarters in San Diego, I was closer to the heart of our operations. But more than the geographical proximity, it was the pulsating ethos of JACK that I felt deeply connected to and in some ways, still do today. I knew that the legacy I was creating was not just about numbers on a balance sheet. It was about creating a community where everyone, from the kitchen staff to the top executives, felt valued, heard, and empowered. Even while recalling these experiences, I can't help but feel a surge of nostalgia and pride. When I joined JACK in the aftermath of the E. coli crisis, the brand needed to pivot, and I was right in the midst of that pivotal transformation. That remains something I am proud of.

We had to make JACK relevant again. We shifted from being perceived as merely an after-bar late-night taco stop to introducing assemble-to-order to fast food, making a mark in the breakfast segment, and offering any product all day. We expanded our target audience, capitalized on our variety of products, brought in healthier options, and seized every opportunity to diversify all aspects of these.

Consistency became my mantra with EGET (every guest, every time). In support of this, I identified two best practices from the restaurant managers in our top performing geographical area and became the champion and sponsor for their system-wide rollout. These two big initiatives were a new grill operating system called "continuous cooking"—which delivered hotter, fresher burgers with less food waste than the old batch cooking system—and a new labor deployment system called "workstation positioning"—which was more efficient, effective, and provided a faster speed of service. On a subsequent employee engagement survey that was administered by our corporate human resources department, these two initiatives were voted by the restaurant managers themselves as the most helpful initiatives in the history of the company.

Consistency and EGET was also complemented by

a range of initiatives like outside order takers, new menu boards, and the voice of the customer. We revamped the brand image with remodels, rebuilds, new designs, and décor. Moreover, we hosted the first-ever restaurant manager conference for all the company and franchise managers, where I emphasized quantum-leap improvements.

Guest focus was central to our transformation. We implemented the "culture under construction" initiative that eventually evolved into Jack's Way. A deep-rooted belief was that the right people—those with a genuine passion for people and service—were essential. It was not just important for our people to meet their goals, but to do so with integrity and care and respect of others. The coveted Jack's Way awards, which I introduced, stood testament to this belief, celebrating those who epitomized the right culture.

We also partnered with Bob Moawad at Edge Learning Institute to further hone our organizational culture. We introduced training programs focusing on self-esteem, positive reinforcement, and leadership with purpose. While I took ownership of the service pillar, collaborations on food and image pillars were crucial. We piloted the entire brand reinvention package in the Seattle market, which included remodeling every restaurant. Engaging all JACK franchisees was a task I passionately undertook.

Building strong teams hinges on understanding and managing diverse sets of skills. For me, the key lies in attracting and nurturing individuals of high caliber. These professionals can accept critique without taking it personally. They operate with skill and humility and will seek out ways to be better instead of waiting for you to tell them.

As a quick side note, high-caliber individuals improve the performance of the leader and the team. So, leaders, don't be afraid of hiring or promoting these people for fear of them outshining or replacing you. Instead, embrace them and let everyone benefit and rise together. I mention this point because I'm sure many of us know or have known people or bosses who are insecure and threatened by high performers. It is my opinion that those people are shortsighted and do not act in the best interest of the team or its broader stakeholders.

My knack for discerning genuine abilities from mere facades is a skill I've honed over the years. To achieve this, I always delve into the essence of what one has accomplished. My inquiries often revolve around probing questions like, "Tell me about a time when . . ." as they reveal not just the person's achievements but their integrity and efficacy.

The performance review, in my eyes, is more than just an evaluation; it's a developmental tool. By offering diverse experiences, such as promoting corporate or staff roles for promising field personnel, or identifying challenging assignments, I aimed to cultivate a culture of growth and development.

A team is only as good as its collective spirit. Bringing the right team together behind a shared vision, fostering an atmosphere of collaboration and open communication, and encouraging diverse views is crucial. Everyone should feel vested in decisions, and once a decision is taken, everyone should own it. That is critical to success. The buck must stop with "us," not just one person. I've always been clear about not having patience for any form of subversive behavior. We are always all in. We win together or lose together. Period.

I should mention, JACK corporate staff had a noticeable "avoid-conflict-at-all-costs" ethos. While overt confrontations were rare, covert disagreements simmered beneath, manifesting in gossip and passive resistance. I championed the cause of open dialogue and constructive debates. My aim was to instill a culture of collective ownership post-decisions, and with time, I began to notice a significant shift in this paradigm, though not fully, in all departments of the company.

But true leadership goes beyond building efficient teams. Respect for a leader is earned through unwavering integrity, active compassion, and consistent performance. You can't just thrive to "do things right," but also to "do the right thing." A leader must also inspire a sense of pride and ownership within the team and foster an environment where members prioritize collective success over individual accolades.

Physical and mental well-being are non-negotiable for a leader. The demands of leadership require resilience. Hence, it's important to prioritize health, seek rejuvenating activities, and maintain a clear mind. Reflecting upon my journey, I take solace in the feedback I've received. People genuinely liked me and wanted to help me succeed, not because I was their boss, but because they respected me and knew I tried to help them succeed.

So, around the mid-2000s, during a conversation with Gerry Fernandez, president of the Multicultural Foodservice & Hospitality Alliance, my views on diversity, equity, and inclusion became a significant talking point. Gerry said he was impressed with how I was able to make such strides in diversity, equity, and inclusion. Then he asked what specific things I did differently to help people of color. He was so deeply moved by my simple response and philosophy that he still tells this story today.

My response to Gerry's question was this: I treat people of color the same as I treat anyone else. I give them the same level of support and opportunity as everyone else, something that historically hasn't been typical in corporate America. Support and opportunities should be distributed equally, regardless of one's background. My belief has always been that talent transcends racial or gender boundaries. If more leaders embraced this philosophy, the organizational landscape would be remarkably diverse.

Our conversation also touched upon the challenging topic of pay inequity, particularly for people of color. Large corporations often have intricate compensation structures, and over time, these can inadvertently perpetuate inequities. Addressing these disparities requires courage, especially given the heightened visibility and potential backlash. Whether it's advocating for mentorship or fighting for pay parity, leaders must be willing to take risks, challenge the status quo, and champion the cause of fairness and equity. I was willing to take the risks.

When Gerry inquired about my approach toward handling those pay disparities concerning minorities, my response was straightforward: "I rectify the inequity." Systems and protocols, including those related to compensation exceptions, exist to address such misalignments. If the affected individual is Black or from any other minority background, my action remains unchanged. I ensure their pay is adjusted rightly, irrespective of potential allegations of favoritism. Because at the core, my decisions aren't dictated by demographics but by the objective principle of fairness. Gerry was an individual supporter of me, my principles, and my career. But everyone is not Gerry. Organizational politics and positioning for power still rule the day.

Whether the cozier ambiance of Jack in the Box or the huge bureaucracy of BP, corporate machinations remained. Politics, treachery, and deceit lurked. While many are above such tactics, some will always try you.

Speaking of trying me, I recall a particular colleague who was a member of a pivotal group and resented my becoming a part of that group. His covert displeasure intensified after I received my next promotion. An incident where he audaciously challenged me in a meeting further crystallized our dynamics. My attempt to privately reconcile differences was met with passive aggression, cementing his role as an undermining backstabber.

I can also recall a colleague who I had to work with on a major project that he had originally wanted to have assigned solely to him. He had hoped to use that opportunity to get a leg up on me for future promotional opportunities. So, once we were both being held accountable for the project's success, and he knew that I was committed to making it a success, he used the situation to slack off and scheme. I could chronicle numerous occasions where I had to carry his load, suffer his betrayals, and endure his inappropriate advances. Instead, it will suffice to say that you should work with integrity and honesty for your rewards and always be careful how you treat others. Unethical behavior is a slippery slope; and life has a way of eventually holding you accountable, as it did with him.

This taught me two incredible lessons. Your camaraderie must be balanced with caution; and your biggest problem may not come from superiors or from those who report to you. Your biggest problems may come from your equals who have an issue with you being their equal.

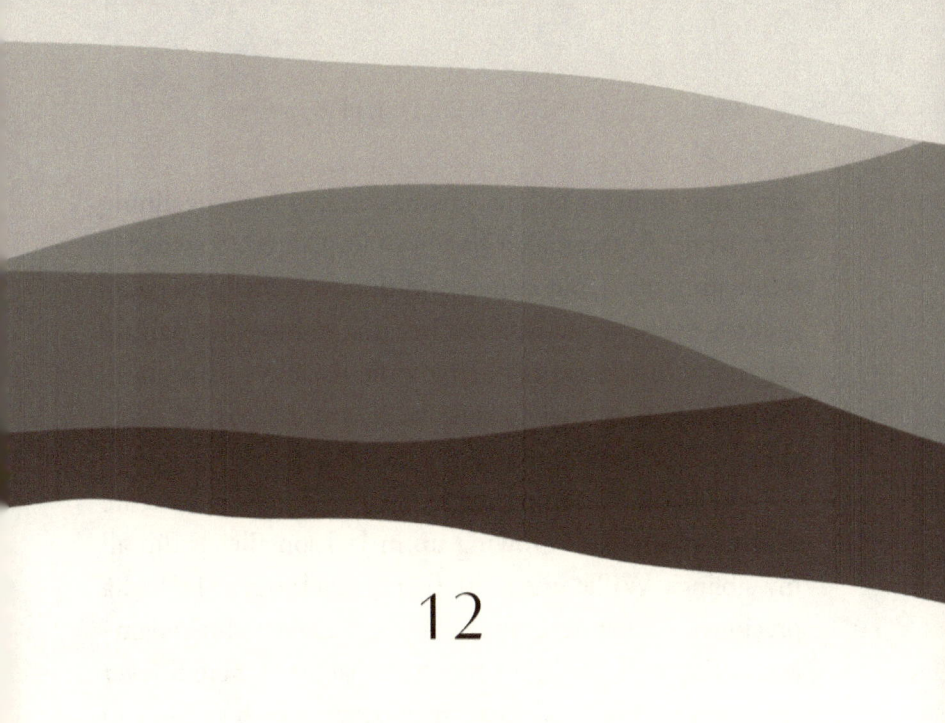

12

Layers

I'm not sure if it's a law, along the line of Murphy's Law, but it might as well be. It seems when so many things are going well, there is always something brewing underneath. I guess there is a reason that even on a bright, sunny day, there are often clouds in the sky as a soft reminder of possible rain.

Not long after I started my new journey with Jack in the Box, I experienced a tragedy. My brother Willie passed away due to heart failure. His health had been declining for a while. A pacemaker had been implanted to assist his weakening heart, but as his condition worsened, the pacemaker's frequent activations became unbearably painful for him. He was experiencing violent kicks to his chest. Eventually they had to remove it, and he passed away shortly after, in the arms of my mother.

His death did something to me. I used to help take care of him when I was growing up in Jacksonville, as did all my siblings. Willie was more than just a brother; he had a precious soul that never fully blossomed. Due to brain damage during childbirth, his mental capabilities were forever cemented in childhood. I had great patience with Willie, and he had a special fondness for me. We loved each other. Not being able to pronounce my name, he called me "Nay-nette."

My mother, who had survived domestic abuse and prison, as well as the deaths of two other sons, her husband, her parents, and her siblings, now had to carry even more pain. It's no wonder that during one of my interviews at JACK, when asked about who I admired the most, I immediately thought of my mother. She was the pinnacle of strength, having taught me to keep believing even in the face of the unbelievable. Life comes at us in layers.

The initial move to Southern California was another layer. While my office, as JACK's LA Region VP, was located in LA County, we strategically decided to reside in Fullerton in Orange County, due to the notorious traffic of Los Angeles. We chose a residence that was still under construction in a beautiful, gated community.

This necessitated a temporary stay in a furnished apartment. We selected an apartment near our new home and in the same school district, in an attempt to minimize the disruption in the lives of our children and their schooling.

Jeanne-Marie found herself uprooted at a pivotal time—her first year of high school. Her initial resentment toward the relocation was palpable. In the end, she blossomed in her new environment. Her academic prowess was complemented by her involvement in cheerleading and creative dance. Her popularity soared, yet it was not without its challenges. Envy and resentment from her peers were obstacles she learned to negotiate. Although still a predominantly white school, I was pleased that there was more diversity at her high school in Fullerton, compared to her previous school in Ohio. My son's elementary school also had a little more diversity, albeit to a lesser extent than the larger high school.

One morning, a routine event took an unexpected turn, forever impacting our lives. It was the day Jeanne-Marie, now sixteen and a licensed driver, first drove to school without a parent. Her little brother, eager to share in this new adventure, accompanied her. They didn't get far. Just outside the front gates, they were hit by another car. Thankfully, they were not seriously injured. However, the family car, a symbol of many journeys and memories, was now a mangled heap of metal.

It appeared that the driver of the other car had left the scene, so in a panic, the kids ran all the way back home and came in the house screaming and crying about what had just happened. We called the police and handled things from there. But the accident affected all of us. It was a stark reminder of life's fragility. Life comes in layers. This accident stirred a deep-seated fear within me, a paranoia rooted in a past tragedy when my brother's life was claimed in an accident, his Volkswagen Bug offering little protection against the merciless force of a collision. This memory, now resurfaced, guided my decision regarding Jeanne-Marie's car. Safety over style—this became my mantra. I would buy her a Mack truck, if necessary. In the end, the car I chose for her, while sturdy and reliable, was not what she had envisioned. A teenager's desire for aesthetics always clashes with a parent's understanding of what is best. We found the middle ground in her senior year, and settled on an SUV, a compromise that brought her joy and me peace of mind. Yet, this joy was short-lived. The SUV, a symbol of her newfound independence, was vandalized at school, a cruel act of jealousy. Ironically, my fear of small cars must have rubbed off on my daughter. To this day, twenty-five years later, my daughter has only owned large SUVs.

While all this was happening, my son, Brad, began coming into his own. In the fourth grade, he expressed a desire for a more challenging academic environment. His request to attend Fairmont Schools, a prestigious National Blue Ribbon private institution, was both shocking and heartening. It was a decision that spoke volumes about his maturity and thirst for knowledge. We embraced his choice, though it meant financial sacrifices. His determination and foresight were qualities we admired and supported wholeheartedly. I often joked that he could one day become the president, such was his charisma and ability to make friends even in the most unlikely places.

Brad's social circle expanded; his friendships included children from diverse and affluent backgrounds. Connections like these afforded him experiences that were both enriching and eye-opening. From private yachts to ranch adventures, his childhood was dotted with extraordinary moments.

A summer camp at Cottontail Ranch, associated with Pepperdine University, was one of the highlights of his young life. There, in a twist of fate, he met and bonded with cousins he had never known. It was a coincidence that defied belief, both our families unknowingly choosing the same camp for our children. This meeting was a reminder of our shared values and aspirations for our children, despite the distance separating us. But remember: Life comes in layers.

During this time of adjustment and new beginnings, sorrow again visited our family. My sister Paula, who had long battled sarcoidosis, succumbed to complications from the disease. Her struggle to breathe, a fight she bravely faced for years, reached its final chapter in a sudden and devastating manner. Rushed to the hospital by our mother, she was sent home only to find herself again gasping for breath, the promised life-saving oxygen machine arriving too late.

Paula declined into a coma. I rushed to the hospital in Jacksonville, joining my other sister and mother in a vigil of grief and disbelief. We then had to make the heart-wrenching decision to disconnect life support. Losing Paula marked the fourth child my mother had to bury.

Her resilience, already tested beyond measure, was once again put to the test.

It was time for a break, but there would be none. In the midst of family tragedies, personal challenges within my own household began to surface. Though it would not be until years later that he was officially diagnosed with ADHD and its associated vulnerability to anxiety and depression, my husband, Michael, grappled with mental health issues. Signs of it began to surface in Ohio, but now it was becoming increasingly evident—mood swings, impulsivity, and an increasing unreliability.

This created an incredible strain on our family. His excessive yelling, especially in my absence, and his dwindling ability to properly execute his responsibilities started to destroy our home. His secret drinking habit, culminating in a DUI, only added to the pressure. The loss of his driving privileges came at a critical time, too, as our son's school was far away, and Michael was primarily responsible for transportation.

Michael loved me and the kids dearly. He would have gladly laid down his life for any of us. And despite how much I loved him, the situation reached a breaking point. In 2000, after the DUI incident, I made the difficult decision to file for divorce. It was a step born not of a lack of love, but from a need to protect our children and my own mental well-being. The realization that his behavior was starting to have a detrimental impact on us all was a painful but necessary acknowledgment.

After I filed for divorce, Michael was diagnosed with

colon cancer. I was numb. Both of us were numb. The diagnosis, amid marital troubles and the passing of siblings, brought a new dimension of complexity I did not know was humanly possible. Opting against the recommended route of a permanent colostomy bag, Michael chose the treatment path of a temporary colostomy bag, radiation, surgery, and chemotherapy. Each step was a battle, both for him and for me. My role shifted from divorcing spouse to loving caregiver, all while still running a two-billion-dollar business and caring for the needs of our two children. Talk about life coming in layers.

I could see the physical and emotional toll on Michael. In June 2001, right in the middle of ongoing challenges, we had to complete our relocation to San Diego. My last promotion with Jack in the Box required that my office be at the corporate headquarters there. The company had allowed us to delay the move until our daughter graduated from high school, and that time had come. We purchased an estate that was still under construction in the Meadows Del Mar. The transition was yet another adjustment for our family, and Michael's health continued to be a central focus. We approached the transition with optimism, despite all the reasons we had to feel negative about it.

Our daughter, now a college student, chose to stay in San Diego for her education, creating an interesting dynamic as she sought independence while we were nearby. Our new home in the grandeur and prestige of the Meadows marked a new chapter in our lives. That said, the challenges in our home were not diminished by the beauty of our surroundings. Getting Michael back to health and attempting to salvage our marriage was an ongoing, daily climb. On the positive side, Michael's health got better, and he was eventually declared cancer-free. But on the negative side, Michael's mental and behavioral challenges continued. In the end, despite all the effort, we still had to divorce. I had to save the pieces of me that were left. The writing had been on the wall, it was just that things were delayed when his sickness took center stage.

Our divorce process was grueling. Still, I was determined to proceed with compassion and fairness. I provided Michael with everything he was entitled to under California law, aiming for a swift and amicable resolution. This included evenly splitting all assets, paying alimony, and covering all legal costs. I also paid child support, despite my son living with me. However, the process dragged on as Michael, driven by hurt and anger, sought additional claims in court. The judge, recognizing the generosity of the initial agreement, dismissed the case. This prolonged battle only added to the stress and heartache of an already painful situation.

When our divorce was finalized, there seemed to be a bit of relief. A new chapter was beginning. Our son remained with me, while our daughter pursued her college education. I was navigating single parenthood and adjusting to life as a single, middle-aged woman, which is an entire book all unto itself.

Reentering the dating scene was complicated beyond measure. The majority of my suitors tended to be very young or significantly older, neither of which I was interested in.

I wanted someone closer to my age. Finding a balance, and someone who was neither intimidated by my success nor resentful of my lifestyle, proved difficult. My home in the Meadows, with its beauty and security measures, often served as an inadvertent barrier to potential relationships.

However, my social circle expanded. I formed close bonds with other families in the Meadows, including four Black families who had moved into the community. Our shared experiences and backgrounds forged strong friendships, offering support and camaraderie in a predominantly white neighborhood. We socialized often and established traditions, such as annual Christmas Eve parties.

Dating brought its share of disappointments and learning experiences. The matchmaking service I tried failed to yield meaningful connections, reflecting the difficulties of dating at my stage of life. Balancing a demanding career, family responsibilities, and a personal life was a continuous juggling act. Life indeed comes in layers.

Our paths crossed unexpectedly, Phillip's and mine. Phillip, who worked for Coca-Cola, had hired my daughter to work part-time as their San Diego State University campus marketing manager. Then one day he saw my daughter and me entering a movie theater at the mall, as he was exiting. He found me attractive and later asked my daughter about who had accompanied her at the mall; and was quite surprised to learn that I was her mother.

Phillip had a subtle approach. Instead of continuing to give her one ticket to the games and events that she had to work at SDSU in the Coca-Cola private viewing room, he would give her two tickets and suggest she bring her mother along. I saw what was going on, but played naive. I was not interested in a relationship with him. But I did enjoy going to the games. Phillip's interactions remained casual and friendly, yet with an undercurrent of something more—unspoken, but palpable.

During one of our conversations, we found that we shared a birth city, our childhoods spent only miles apart. The revelation of our parallel lives made me curious as to why our paths hadn't crossed before. I volunteered that I graduated from Raines High in 1975 and asked him what year and from what school he graduated. He replied that he graduated from Paxton High in 1988, and the mystery was instantly solved. Phillip, younger by a significant measure, was just entering the school system after I had headed off to college.

Learning of his age helped me pour concrete on our platonic boundary. Phillip, however, persisted in what he termed a quest for friendship. His efforts, while respectful, hinted at deeper desires. Friends and acquaintances noticed, often remarking on his obvious affection for me. I continued to navigate these waters, embracing his friendship, while maintaining a boundary to romance. It turned out to be a dangerous balance.

Phillip's kindness and thoughtfulness started to break up that concrete. His patience was unwavering. For nearly two years, he remained a steadfast presence in my life, a friend in whom I found comfort and reliability.

The narrative of our relationship took an unexpected

turn during a Jack in the Box Senior Leadership Team's annual holiday celebration. I invited Phillip to be my escort that year because I thought he would be a safe choice, without romantic complications. The event, grand in its execution, offered incredible food and wine. It was an evening of elegance and joy, on many levels.

Too much wine clouded my usual restraint, and in that unguarded moment, our relationship erased the boundaries of friendship. Phillip's kiss—tender and passionate—fed something in me that was starving. That night marked the beginning of a profound, passionate journey. We became inseparable. Still, I wrestled with doubts.

Our age gap and my recent divorce both kept a small part of my heart closed. The financial disparity between us added another layer of complexity. Several times I attempted to sever ties, convinced that a future together was impossible. But he persisted. We addressed our concerns with candid discussions, setting a foundation of transparency and mutual respect. I started to believe we did have a future after all.

The foundation of our friendship was powerful. We would hike, walk along the ocean, swim, travel, cruise, all of it. Our culinary adventures ranged from intimate home-cooked meals to dining out, followed by nights of dancing. Hours spent in the hot tub or by the firepit were filled with conversations and shared dreams. He was an emotional rock for me, at a time when I desperately needed one. In the end, I fell deeply in love with him.

As my life with Phillip evolved, my past was not left untouched. Michael, my first husband, harbored resentment and anger toward me following our divorce. It was not until about two years later that he approached me with a newfound understanding. He had sought therapy to deal with our divorce and during the process he was diagnosed with ADHD with anxiety and depression and had begun proper treatment. He apologized to me for all he had put me through and told me that he appreciated me standing by him all those years and all I had done for him and our children. We then began to rebuild a friendship, rooted in mutual respect and shared history. Our interactions became more cordial, especially during family events involving our children. Michael even extended invitations to Phillip and me, which we accepted, to watch his and his girlfriend's zydeco band perform, a gesture of acceptance and goodwill.

However, life dealt Michael a cruel hand. His battle with cancer, which had once seemed conquered, returned with a vengeance, spreading to multiple organs. He sought various treatments, traveling as far as Asia in search of healing. Witnessing his struggle, I grappled with complex emotions, a mix of past hurts and present sympathies. Life comes in layers.

During these years, my daughter was enjoying college life. Although she didn't live at home, it was truly wonderful to have her in the same city. Getting to frequently spend mother-daughter time with her was a highlight in my life. The first year when she was living in a dorm, it would warm my heart to wake up on a Saturday and see that she had come over to do her laundry and shop in my pantry, like it was Walmart. 😊 I used to tease her. But I loved it. I treasured our dining-out rituals, especially sharing the Great Wall of Chocolate dessert at P.F. Chang's. And most important was knowing that I could get to her quickly if she needed my help. In 2005 she graduated college and accepted a job offer in Atlanta. We had a lovely party and dinner celebration for her, hosted at our home. Family and friends from near and far attended. It was a wonderful time. But remember those layers.

My mother was not able to attend the graduation or the celebrations. Shortly before then, having already been through inconceivable hardships in her life, my mother suffered a debilitating stroke, necessitating round-the-clock care in a nursing facility. Her condition was a stark contrast to the strong, independent woman I had always known. My sister Dee and I shouldered the responsibility of managing her care, alternating visits to Jacksonville. These coast-to-coast trips, coupled with my extensive work travel, took a physical and emotional toll.

The sight of my once-formidable mother, now confined and unresponsive, was heart-wrenching. Concurrently, grappling with Michael's worsening health compounded my emotional burden. It felt like a relentless onslaught of sorrow and challenge. Phillip, sensing the weight of these responsibilities, began accompanying me on visits to see my mother. She responded to his presence with a brightness that was rare in those days. His support during this time was more than I could have ever asked for.

Tragically, my mother passed away in early January

2006, just days after our last visit. The process of handling her affairs was another journey, one filled with reflection and grief.

Amid this turmoil, my son, Brad, was involved in a serious car accident while I was visiting my mother. The news, delivered by Michael, was a jarring reminder of life's unpredictability. Thankfully, Brad escaped with minor injuries, but the incident reminded me again of my little brother's tragic death. The scars are still there.

I was always so deeply concerned about the toll that all the family deaths must have had on my mother. Yet, it was not until after my mother's death that I honestly faced the realization that my sister Dee and I had both suffered through all of these same losses—four siblings, both grandparents, both aunts, and now both parents—and also carried these great scars and burdens of grief, which we never fully dealt with. I also carried the grief of the loss of a twenty-four-year marriage and would soon have to grieve the death of this same man I loved who was the father of my children.

And as if there weren't enough accidents in my family, in 2006 I was involved in a major one myself that would have taken my life had I not been contained by the safe craftsmanship of Mercedes-Benz. Prior to my car accident, I paid lip service to saying life is short and you've got to slow down and smell the roses. Even after the death of both my aunts and four siblings, while still in their forties or younger, I continued to pay lip service. I didn't change my life or slow down my intense pace. But after my accident, after realizing I survived due to God and German engineering, things changed. This incident became a catalyst for introspection, leaving me with lasting physical and emotional scars.

Also, during those years, I started suffering with migraines. I didn't fully understand until a few years later that they were being primarily triggered by food and environmental allergies. But at the time, it was another factor of concern for my health. At some point, I sat down and had to ask myself, *Where do I go from here?* Those years had been nothing short of an avalanche. My body was screaming at me to do something different. The weight of stress that younger Gladys could carry without blinking now required all the strength I could muster.

I no longer had tolerance for political bull crap. I needed a break. In 2007 I had surgery on my cervical spine, accepted Phillip's marriage proposal, quit my job at Jack in the Box, and took time out to heal, both physically and emotionally. My physical healing required almost a full year of wearing a space-like (or terrorist-style) bone-healing stimulator machine around my neck (even while sleeping).

Also in 2007, my daughter got engaged, had a destination wedding, and moved to Asia. Additionally, my son, Brad, graduated from high school. Again, friends and family came to celebrate the occasion with us. My fiftieth birthday was also within days of his graduation. This, too, was a momentous occasion in our family. My sister Dee and I had made promises to each other that we would celebrate big-time when each of us reached the age of fifty, given our family history. Unbelievably, none of our other four blood siblings, or our mother's siblings, had lived beyond their forties.

So, while my closest people were in town for my son's graduation, I started my celebration by having an amazingly "pimped out" stretch limousine drive us for a visit and dinner celebration in Temecula wine country, and later Phillip and I flew on to the Atlantis Paradise Island Bahamas for a spectacular stay.

After a year of healing and reenergizing, I accepted a position on the Global Executive Team of Burger King in Miami, Florida. It was the start of yet another layer.

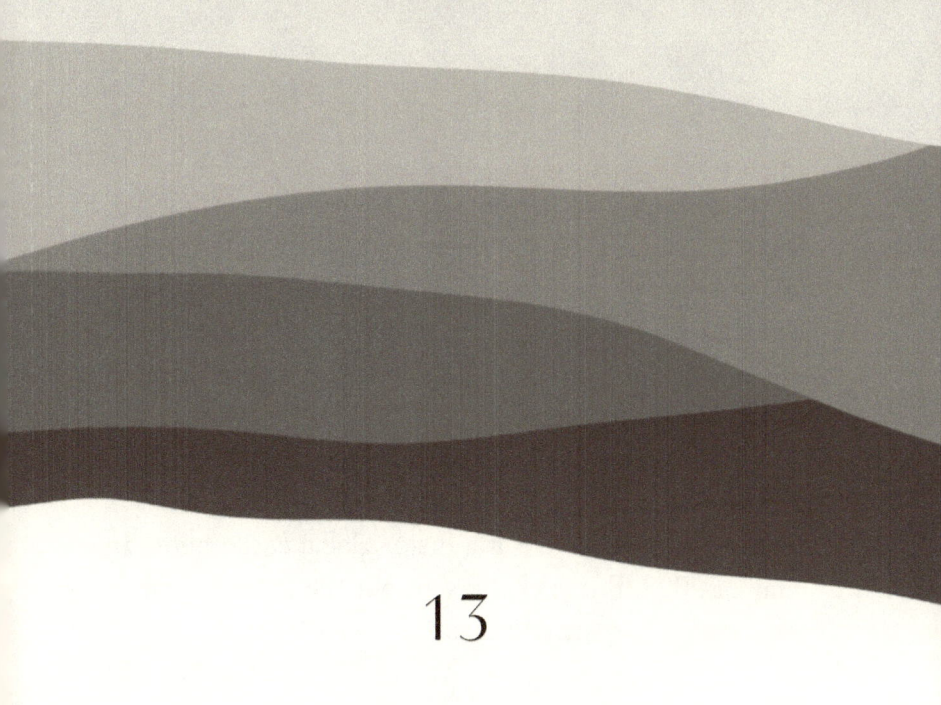

13

Have It Your Way

When the king calls, you answer—Burger King, that is. It seems change encourages more change, and random causes more random to happen. My journey from one industry to another had one more surprise, and that was thrusting me into the "Have It Your Way" organization as senior vice president of North America operations. For me, and for anyone who looks like me, this was huge.

I say "huge" because since 1955, when the Fortune 500 list was created, there have been more than 1,800 C-level executives at the helm, running one of the list's legendary companies. Only nineteen have been Black and only six of the nineteen have been Black women, a percentage of 0.003, for those keeping score.

While I was not the CEO of Burger King, this simply provides context as to the rarified air of being a Black female senior executive at a major global corporation. In May of 2008, Burger King sent out the following press release signaling my entrance.

> *Burger King Corp. (NYSE: BKC) yesterday announced the appointment of Gladys DeClouet as senior vice president, North America company operations. DeClouet succeeds Dave Gagnon, who announced his intention to leave the company at the end of the fiscal year. DeClouet will be responsible for all operations and the profitability of the US and Canadian company-owned restaurants. She reports to Chuck Fallon, president, North America.*
>
> *Gladys is the former vice president of operations for Jack in the Box. In this role, Gladys had responsibility for over 900 company-operated restaurants and $1.8 billion in sales. She also oversaw the operations of Jack in the Box's company-owned Quickstuff-branded convenience store and fuel locations. Prior to joining Jack in the Box, Gladys worked for British Petroleum Inc., holding a number of positions of increasing responsibility in marketing, distribution, planning, finance, and*

business development. Earlier in her career, she was an engineer with Conoco Inc., working in offshore oil and gas exploration and production.

DeClouet says, "I am glad to be joining the Burger King North American team in its new era of growth. I am confident that my past experiences in developing and managing great teams will enable us to build upon the recent successes in sales expansion, through strategic initiatives including new company restaurant openings, reimaging efforts, and the delivery of exceptional guest service."

Gladys holds a master's in business administration in finance and investment banking from the University of Wisconsin at Madison, and a bachelor's in mechanical engineering from Tuskegee University. A native of Jacksonville, Florida, Gladys and her family will return to Florida and reside in Miami.

My return to Florida is a story all unto its own, but first let me finish the Burger King story. Burger King Corporation is a restaurant company specializing in flame-broiled hamburgers. It is the world's second-largest fast-food hamburger chain. During my tenure, it had over fourteen billion dollars in revenues (twenty-seven billion in 2025 dollars) and operated nearly 14,000 restaurants in fifty states and nearly one hundred countries and US territories. Historically, it had also gone through multiple ownership changes with non-restaurant companies and investor groups. First it was in the hands of Pillsbury in 1967, followed by a transfer of power to the British titan Grand Metropolitan

(Grand Met) PLC in 1989. Then a merger with Irish brewer Guinness PLC gave birth to Diageo PLC in 1997; until finally the company landed in the arms of a consortium of private equity financiers in 2002. Also, Burger King had recently reacquired several hundred of their US restaurants from various franchisees.

Each transaction left an imprint. Diverse corporate cultures had molded it into a gold mine of opportunities that needed to be unearthed. Burger King was seeking the right individual to breathe life into its valuable, but somewhat disjointed, empire.

There I was, chosen to lead the transformation, entrusted with the mission to resurrect a giant. I was not just tasked to lead, unify, and improve the performance of its North America Company Operations, which accounted for more than a third of its global profit. I was also expected to forge a path that would inspire franchisees globally, sharing best practices and painting a vision not just of a fast-food giant, but of a dynamic, responsive entity ready to cater to the next generation of burger enthusiasts.

Stepping into this role, I harbored no illusions. The task was monumental. I had to integrate a mosaic of legacies into a cohesive, forward-moving culture. However, this wasn't my first dance. From creating synergy at Conoco and BP among many who didn't want me there, to walking into JACK after one of the worst food-safety nightmares America had ever seen—conquering immense challenges is what I do.

I joined Burger King in early 2008. I increased sales

and profits in company-owned restaurants during the worst economic downturn in the US since the Great Depression, while also facing intense competitor discounting. My initial operational challenges were quite different from those at Jack in the Box. But my approach to the people and the building of a culture of care and respect, inclusiveness, service-profit chain philosophy, and accountability was the same. A few of my accomplishments were:

- Improved company restaurant margin 13 percent in one year

- Led significant improvements in: caliber and capability of management team; reimaging, repair, and maintenance of facilities; and overall guest satisfaction as surveyed by our guests

- Established a culture of cost and financial control throughout the organization, including development and enforcement of national inventory and cash handling policies and procedures

- Led collaborative and smooth acquisition and refranchising deals, including the successful integration of Burger King's single largest franchise acquisition of four hundred-plus restaurants into company operations

- Perfect "5" rating on most recent performance review in both categories: Leader of change; and Executes against priorities

- 360-degree feedback report by peers, subordinates, and superiors rated the following as my Top 5 Executive Competencies: Takes initiative; Treats all people right; Knows the business; Invests wisely; and Communicates effectively

- Featured on cover of *Black Enterprise* magazine, February 2009, and throughout article on the "100 Most Powerful Executives in Corporate America"

- Featured by *Black Enterprise* magazine, February 2010, as one of "Most Powerful Women in Business"

- Greater Miami Chamber of Commerce: Board of Governor's Member

- *Profiles in Diversity* journal, 2011, "Women Worth Watching" award winner

My three years with Burger King can be characterized by two distinct phases. The initial one was a period of dynamic camaraderie and enjoyment coupled with hard work, where we united to lift the company to new heights. We laughed, brainstormed freely, marked personal milestones, and created bonds that were more like familial than working relationships. We embraced a culture where hard work and fun seamlessly blended, creating an environment that drove our daily endeavors.

The second phase emerged without warning, brought on by the purchase of Burger King by the Brazilian private equity firm 3G Capital. The lively environment of our workplace began to dim as we entered a stage of change, and eventually saying goodbye to a place that had been a substantial part of our lives. I can recall the mood shift during our quarterly Global Executive Team meeting when we were told of the upcoming acquisition by 3G, and informed that all of us GET members would ultimately be displaced with the acquisition.

As the reality of the upcoming shifts started to materialize, I couldn't help but look back on our shared voyage, from the sessions where we conceived innovative strategies to private celebrations of personal milestones. I remembered the successful Star Trek marketing venture, where as a fun part of the internal celebration, they made larger-than-life-sized stand-up images of the Star Trek characters, but with the heads of our GET members on the bodies. So cute and creative. It seemed it was all over so fast.

I remained optimistic, wishing the best for every individual who had been a part of this fantastic journey. Oh, but I do need to uncover some of the personal elements that were at play during this move back to Florida.

I had left northern Florida in 1975 and only returned, it seemed, for illnesses and funerals. In 2008, this born-and-raised Floridian was coming to her home state. But this time as a professional, and to Miami of all places. Miami is referred to as its own international country, as opposed to a US city. For people who don't know much about Miami or who never saw *Scarface*, it is a melting pot culture—a mix of Cuban, South American, Haitian, other Caribbean,

European, and so on. It is the only US city founded by a woman, Julia Tuttle. Miami hosts fourteen million tourists a year and is the US's warmest city in the winter (65-75 degrees Fahrenheit). It is a wonderful city, most of the time. But there were some major things that happened, much of which had little to do with working for the King.

At the end of 2009, given the toll that losing his dad was having on my son, we decided to have Brad move from San Diego to Miami and complete his remaining two years of college at the University of Miami. Having him here allowed me to provide him additional support and was good for both of us.

At the beginning of 2011, my signing of a noncompete agreement, as a result of the Burger King buyout, coincided with a significant family move. My daughter relocated to the Miami/Ft. Lauderdale area, a change caused by her husband's career. These events presented the opportunity for me to spend more time with my daughter, two very young granddaughters, and son-in-law, in addition to my husband. So, I planned to delay another career move for a year or two. But remember those layers.

During my sabbatical, a regular workout session resulted in a lumbar spine injury, propelling me into a temporary life on wheels and a sequence of painful surgeries. The very notion of returning to work, once an exciting idea, temporarily became an impossibility because of pain and recovery.

Compounding these personal events, change uprooted us once more. Phillip's company restructured, necessitating a relocation to Atlanta. Adapting to a new city was challenging. Neither of us liked living in Atlanta. Consequently, we found ourselves homeowners of two residences, straddling the space between a professional necessity and a personal haven on the beach in South Florida. I began to look at my professional future through a different lens, and started to consider my professional work as coming to a permanent end.

Since departing from my former role, life has been a mosaic of challenges and triumphs. My journey has been marked by additional surgeries, chronic pain, and personal loss. Nonetheless, there has been beauty and growth. I have witnessed my granddaughters transform into remarkable young women and have sustained my lifelong commitment to fitness. I still look much younger than my age and work out at a consistent pace. Freed from the constraints of a professional schedule, I relish my new life and live with gratitude each day. I am constantly reminded of the grace that has and will continue to sustain me. God allows me to savor precious moments, something I will never take for granted.

14

What Really Matters

" I want to be the top executive of a major global corporation."
That was the first sentence of my essay. It was written while applying for graduate school scholarships.
We were directed to compose an essay detailing what we desired to do with our education. This is how I answered.
I wanted to be at the top of the top.

I received scholarships for the two years while in my

MBA program. Each time, I continued to proclaim my intent to be the global head of a major corporation. But I must say, during my first few years at BP, the second-largest oil company in the world, my tone began to change. After meeting and learning about the men who passed through to that top position, and the ones desperately seeking that position, I concluded that there wasn't enough money in the whole damn world to make me sacrifice my family and my very soul, in pursuit of that or any other goal.

That may sound overly dramatic, and there are some clichés that are blown out of proportion. But climbing to the top of one of the world's largest corporations is about as close to a soul-selling endeavor as one would ever care to get. For me, there was simply more to life, like precious moments with your spouse, watching your children grow, and being a person of integrity. It is an interesting balance, however. On one hand, you must give your energy and time to your profession; on the other hand, you can never redeem the time lost with your loved ones. There is a significant cost to success, and at some point, you have to decide what you are willing to pay.

All of this reveals itself over time. Life really does come in layers, each laid upon the previous, a chorus of lessons learned, hardships endured, and joys experienced. Every element has carved its mark on my journey. I am proud to say, I never lost sight of what really matters.

Corporate life is a windstorm. Flights to catch, meetings to facilitate, budgets to approve. Years, even decades go by in the blink of an eye. It is only when the activity slows, only when reflection is your morning routine, that one can truly analyze what has happened all these years.

During moments of reflection, I think about the many roles I've played—the executive, the partner, the matriarch. My life's work, illustrious to onlookers, has been anything but simple. It was a mosaic of every emotion woven together with tenacity and resilience, but also with strands of undue pressure and unspoken expectations.

I often tell friends that for some reason, those around me have always believed I was not human. It sounds funny, but it's true. People always believed I was Superwoman, and it almost killed me. Have you ever been called by a family member to rally around another loved one who needs support? But while you're listening to the other person's problems, you're thinking, "That's me. I'm in the same position. Who is going to make the calls and gather support for me?" That mentality carries over from the home to the office to the executive suite.

I fully understand. High-performing professionals get things done. That's the long and short of it. I can't tell you how many times I have heard someone mention that a certain task was too stressful for them, so they wanted me to do it. Being Superwoman is dangerous. It brings super illness, super stress, and causes super divorces. The reality is that Superwoman is fictional—and so is Superman, for that matter. A person can be Super Exceptional. But they need help and support to live a happy, balanced life, especially for women. Even now, decades into the twenty-first century, most working women still carry the lion's share of domestic and child-rearing responsibility, in addition to their careers.

If I had written this book years ago, I probably would not say half of the things I am saying now, but there is something about time. Time lets you know how little you have left. It teaches you that so much of what you did to keep everyone else comfortable are the same things that rob you of a restful night's sleep. It helps you better understand yourself.

For some corporate executives, their career or position is their identity. Without that, they lose their sense of purpose and self-worth. But this is not the case for me. I find my self-worth and identity through my relationships with loved ones; and making positive contributions to the future and lives of others. Once I was no longer in corporate America, I didn't mourn the loss of a career. I felt proud of my contributions as a trailblazer, role model, and mentor who opened doors for so many behind me. I felt incredibly blessed to have more time to spend with the people I love—my family and friends.

Through illness—my own and that of others—and through the recognition of life's inherent fragility, I humbly concluded that no company, regardless of my dedication to it, will be present in my final, solitary moments.

In the end, the most important layer of life itself is that sacred covering—family.

Acknowledgments

I would like to express my deepest thanks to:

God, first and foremost, for providing grace and favor in my life, and giving me the strength to face and overcome my trials and tribulations.

My sister Dee, for her love and support and being there for me throughout my life.

My children, Jeanne-Marie and Bradford, for the joy, honor, and pride of being their mother, and for their encouragement and support for me to write this book and share my story. Also, my granddaughters, for being my inspiration and giving me the courage to tell my story, in hopes of inspiring other young ladies like them.

All my other family and friends (you know who you are) who have loved and supported me throughout my journey. You celebrated my victories and stood by me during the tough times. I appreciate you. You are everything!

Finally, thanks to every one of you who took the time to read this book. I truly appreciate you and hope you found benefit in doing so.

Author Photograph by Llobet Photography

About the Author

Gladys H. DeClouet is a former senior executive with an exceptional record of running multibillion-dollar businesses. She forged a pioneer path through the oil and restaurant industries. She led divisions at major corporations, such as British Petroleum, Burger King, and Jack in the Box, to financial growth and strategic success. Gladys began her professional career with Conoco Oil as the first female engineer in offshore oil and gas exploration and production and continued to open doors as the first female or first Black female to achieve positions throughout her career. Gladys is a respected leader, recognized for her integrity and ability to attract and develop superior and diverse teams. She is passionate about mentoring and sharing her knowledge and experience with others.

Her influence extends beyond business achievements, as evidenced by her features in *Black Enterprise* magazine, where she was recognized among the most powerful executives and women in business. Her educational background includes an MBA in finance and investment banking from the University of Wisconsin-Madison and a BS in mechanical engineering from Tuskegee University. Actively involved in her community, she has served on several boards. She enjoys music, dancing, and traveling, integrating personal passions with a profound professional legacy. Gladys has since retired and lives in her home state of Florida.